LEARNING TO LEAD
— *with* —
NEHEMIAH

A 25 Day Bible Study on the Rebuilding of the Walls of Jerusalem

j44 MEDIA   W⬤RITAL

CONTENTS

INTRODUCTION

For many years, I read through the book of Nehemiah routinely as part of a practice of reading through the Bible. It has always been fascinating, and I read it with an appreciation of a good story. A few years ago, I was asked to write a single day study on the book, and as I studied, I discovered the hidden gems in Nehemiah. Over the years, I have returned to this book and every time I have learned so much that applies to my life as a Christian and to my walk as a leader. I would like to invite you to fall in love with this book with me and gather nuggets to help in your everyday lives.

I have restricted this study to the first six chapters, covering the rebuilding of the walls of Jerusalem. Using a selection of verses, I share my thoughts and observations on these verses with you along with Scriptures that help to illustrate some truths I discuss. I did not intend for this to be a deep theological work with expositions in Greek and Hebrew. It's a glimpse into what God opened my eyes to see as I mulled these verses in my heart. You may notice a business bent to some of my thoughts. I will simply say it's a hazard of my day job and I hope it illustrates how relevant the Word of God is, even now.

One thing that helps me remember what I study is trying to summarize it in my words. I asked myself a question—if I could summarize what I learned in these verses into one word, what would it be and why? The result of this is the 'Word of the Day" which I hope gives you a quick summary to remind yourself during your day. As I mentioned, these are words I came up with so feel free to come up with your own! There is no wrong answer here!

The beauty of studying God's Word is God highlights different things to each one of us. Take some time to ponder on what God is saying to you specifically with the verses you read so that this becomes a personal word for you. I invite you to write down what God is dealing with you about and follow His instructions. Let God speak to you about fears, attitudes, heights, and victories ahead. Let Him open your eyes to see the great vision He created for you to accomplish. Most importantly, I pray you are encouraged to take a step of faith and do what God has laid on your heart.

CAUSE AND EFFECT

The LORD, the God of their ancestors, sent word to them through his messengers again and again, because he had pity on his people and on his dwelling place. But they mocked God's messengers, despised his words and scoffed at his prophets until the wrath of the LORD was aroused against his people and there was no remedy. He brought up against them the king of the Babylonians, who killed their young men with the sword in the sanctuary, and did not spare young men or young women, the elderly or the infirm. God gave them all into the hands of Nebuchadnezzar. He carried to Babylon all the articles from the temple of God, both large and small, and the treasures of the LORD's temple and the treasures of the king and his officials. They set fire to God's temple and broke down the wall of Jerusalem; they burned all the palaces and destroyed everything of value there.

He carried into exile to Babylon the remnant, who escaped from the sword, and they became servants to him and his successors until the kingdom of Persia came to power. The land enjoyed its sabbath rests; all the time of its desolation it rested, until the seventy years were completed in fulfillment of the word of the LORD spoken by Jeremiah.

In the first year of Cyrus king of Persia, in order to fulfill the word of the LORD spoken by Jeremiah, the LORD moved the heart of Cyrus king of Persia to make a proclamation throughout his realm and also to put it in writing: "This is what Cyrus king of Persia says: "'The LORD, the God of heaven, has given me all the kingdoms of the earth and he has appointed me to build a temple for him at Jerusalem in Judah. Any of his people among you may go up, and may the LORD their God be with them.'"
-2 Chronicles 36:15-23

To fully understand the story of Nehemiah, I think it's important to provide the back story to the times he was living in. To add some color, we pick up the story from the end of 2 Chronicles and through Ezra to understand what brought the Israelites into exile in Babylon.

The children of Israel had sinned against the Lord. Despite multiple warnings, they did not repent until their cup of mercy ran dry. They could not imagine God would allow the nation that bore His name to be sent to captivity. Over time, Nebuchadnezzar attacked Jerusalem and razed it. The great temple Solomon built was destroyed. The ark of the covenant was missing. Everything that distinguished Israel from her surrounding countries was no longer in existence. Like we can all testify, there are real consequences for going against God's will.

As God had promised, the children of Israel spent seventy years in captivity in Babylon until Cyrus became king and started the first wave of migration to Jerusalem. About forty-two thousand people returned to Jerusalem under Zerubbabel's leadership. Their goal was to rebuild the temple so that the worship of God would be reinstated. They came with resources of gold and silver to restore the temple to its former glory—a process fraught with challenges and ultimately took about twenty years to complete.

Many years later, Ezra would lead another team of about fifteen hundred back to Jerusalem. Ezra had been given a mandate to teach the people of Israel God's laws. The king had recognized it was not enough to worship in the temple at appointed times. The Israelites needed to know the laws of God and live by them. Ezra encountered the people who either did not know the laws of God or had abandoned them.

The very things that made the nation of Israel unique seemed to be missing, and they could not get it back. Their glory was the temple which was now severely diminished. They had lost the ark of the covenant, which signified God's presence. The Levites and priests were not well versed in their way of worship. They seemed to have lost their protection from God. The blessing of God was no longer evident. This was the state of Israel before Nehemiah, a contemporary of Ezra, came on the scene.

In spite of the struggles the children of Israel had, one thing became clear—God had not abandoned them. So remember when the world is throwing things at you, and it seems God is silent, He has not abandoned you either. He is working behind the scenes to restore you even from self-imposed destruction.

"'The LORD bless you and keep you; the LORD make his face shine on you and be gracious to you; the LORD turn his face toward you and give you peace.' 'So they will put my name on the Israelites, and I will bless them.'"
-Numbers 6:24-27

"'For I know the plans I have for you,' declares the LORD, 'plans to prosper you and not to harm you, plans to give you hope and a future.'"
-Jeremiah 29:11

"But you are a chosen people, a royal priesthood, a holy nation, God's special possession, that you may declare the praises of him who called you out of darkness into his wonderful light. Once you were not a people, but now you are the people of God; once you had not received mercy, but now you have received mercy."

-1 Peter 2:9-10

— Word of the Day —
IDENTITY

The qualities of a person or group that make them different from others[1]. The children of Israel had their identity as the chosen nation, and this was evident in their relationship with God, their way of worship, and their obedience to the law. Whenever they stopped pursuing their relationship with God, they lost their identity and became fair game for their enemies who were stronger than them. As a believer, my identity is tied to my relationship with God and evidenced in my worship and study of His Word. I cannot afford to conform to our environment and then lose the identity I have in God.

— What is God saying to me now? —

Where do I find my identity? What things define me?

. . . .

. . . .

. . . .

. . . .

. . . .

. . . .

. . . .

. . . .

. . . .

. . . .

. . . .

. . . .

. . . .

. . . .

. . . .

. . . .

. . . .

. . . .

. . . .
. . . .
. . . .
. . . .
. . . .
. . . .
. . . .
. . . .
. . . .
. . . .
. . . .
. . . .
. . . .
. . . .
. . . .
. . . .
. . . .
. . . .
. . . .
. . . .
. . . .
. . . .
. . . .

DAY TWO

STILL RUBBLE

Nehemiah's Prayer
The words of Nehemiah, son of Hakaliah:

In the month of Kislev in the twentieth year, while I was in the citadel of Susa, Hanani, one of my brothers, came from Judah with some other men, and I questioned them about the Jewish remnant that had survived the exile, and also about Jerusalem. They said to me, "Those who survived the exile and are back in the province are in great trouble and disgrace. The wall of Jerusalem is broken down, and its gates have been burned with fire."
-Nehemiah 1:1-3

Have you ever been in a place where your expectation is so far from your reality? You have done everything you are supposed to, met every requirement, but the results simply do not add up to what you would have predicted. If yes, then you can understand some emotions Nehemiah goes through with this report from Jerusalem. The Jewish remnant had returned to Jerusalem with great fanfare and high expectations. They were going back to rebuild the city. They were returning based on the promise God gave Jeremiah, a promise that after their time of exile, they would be restored.

"This is what the LORD says: 'I will restore the fortunes of Jacob's tents and have compassion on his dwellings; the city will be rebuilt on her ruins, and the palace will stand in its proper place. From them will come songs of thanksgiving and the sound of rejoicing. I will add to their numbers, and they will not be decreased; I will bring them honor, and they will not be disdained.'"
-Jeremiah 30:18-19

These faithful few took God at His word and returned to Jerusalem to rebuild the temple and city. They returned to a place where they could serve God in freedom, to an inheritance they could call their own. But alas, their expectation did not meet up with their reality.

Hanani reports the remnants were in great trouble and disgrace. They were in great trouble—in great difficulty, in a dangerous situation. There was no protection from enemies. They lived in a constant state of fear and vulnerability. There was no way to amass wealth because it could easily be stolen. There was no opportunity to let their guard down. They were in great trouble! They were also in disgrace. These people who were called by the name of the Most High could not even afford to rebuild the walls of the city. The new temple that had been rebuilt paled in comparison to the old. The city was destroyed and despite the passage of time and what we believe must have been a lot of attempts to rebuild, *"The wall of Jerusalem is still rubble; the city gates are still cinders." (Nehemiah 1:3 MSG)*

Many years ago, I sold my possessions and left all that was familiar to pursue a masters in the United States. I had received a word from the Lord that He would provide for my masters, and I took a great leap of faith to pursue my dreams. As time went by, my resources dwindled, and I could not see a path forward to raising the money I needed. I was in great trouble, and ahead of me was the prospect of returning home in disgrace.

But my story did not end there. Just like me, the children of Israel did not know God had already turned their situation around. In faraway Babylon, God was raising a Nehemiah to provide direction and help rebuild the wall.

Are there walls in your life that are still rubble? Are there things you fully expected to have moved further than they have now? Are you dealing with some trouble or something giving you cause for shame? Remind yourself there is more to the story than you have seen so far. God will forever be faithful to His word. He is the very definition of integrity, and you can trust His word.

"Why, my soul, are you downcast? Why so disturbed within me? Put your hope in God, for I will yet praise him, my Savior and my God."
-Psalm 42:5

"Instead of your shame you will receive a double portion, and instead of disgrace you will rejoice in your inheritance. And so you will inherit a double portion in your land, and everlasting joy will be yours."
-Isaiah 61:7

"There is surely a future hope for you, and your hope will not be cut off."
-Proverbs 23:18

"Let us hold unswervingly to the hope we profess, for he who promised is faithful."
-Hebrews 10:23

—— **Word of the Day** ——

OPPORTUNITY

A good chance for advancement or progress[2]. Anytime expectations do not match reality, we have an opportunity. An opportunity for God to work miracles and to do great things in and through me. An opportunity for growth, innovation, for ministry. Anytime expectations do not match reality, we have a good chance for advancement or progress.

— **What is God saying to me now?** —

What trouble or disgrace am I currently facing that can become opportunities?

....

....

....

....

....

....

....

....

....

....

....

....

....

....

....

....

....

....

THINGS THAT BREAK YOUR HEART

When I heard these things, I sat down and wept. For some days I mourned and fasted and prayed before the God of heaven. Then I said: "Lord, the God of heaven, the great and awesome God, who keeps his covenant of love with those who love him and keep his commandments, let your ear be attentive and your eyes open to hear the prayer your servant is praying before you day and night for your servants, the people of Israel. I confess the sins we Israelites, including myself and my father's family, have committed against you. We have acted very wickedly toward you. We have not obeyed the commands, decrees and laws you gave your servant Moses.
  -Nehemiah 1:4-7

Whenever I read about the sorrow Nehemiah displayed over the Israelites living in Jerusalem, a few things jump out to me. First, Nehemiah sat down and wept. So many times, we equate tears with an absence of faith.

I don't want to gloss over the fact you have permission to weep. The Bible teaches that we should *"rejoice with those who rejoice; mourn with those who mourn" (Romans 12:15).* We shouldn't shame people for weeping when we should really weep with them. There is *"a time to weep and a time to laugh, a time to mourn and a time to dance!" (Ecclesiastes 3:4).*

Another thing I marvel at is Nehemiah's compassion. When did I last mourn for the plight of someone not directly related to me? I don't know about you, but most of the time that I mourn or fast, it's because something has directly impacted me or someone close to me. I am saddened when I read about wars and atrocities in different places, but rarely am I moved to the depth of emotion displayed here. I would pray the famous prayer by World Vision's founder Bob Pierce: "Let my heart be broken with the things that break the heart of God," and wait for my heart to be broken over something big or noble.

I have come to realize my heart will not be broken by everything. Those things that actually touch my emotions (anger, sorrow, fear), indicate what God wants me to intercede about and, in many cases, what God wants me to do something about. God may not use me to bring about world peace, but what He draws my attention to is important.

We are built to notice different things from others. Pay attention to what breaks your heart as this is key to fulfilling your purpose

Beyond the emotions, I think it's important to focus on Nehemiah's actions. He didn't stay weeping; he laid the situation before God. He went to the One who could do something about it. In this age of activism and social justice, it's the norm to fight with social media and leave it all there. Nehemiah took time out to seek God's face for strategy and instruction before going on to "do the impossible."

Lastly, I want to draw your attention to how Nehemiah prayed. Here we see the heart of an intercessor. Nehemiah put himself in their shoes. He didn't say, "God, these people have sinned." He included himself and his father's house. Though he was safe and comfortable in the king's palace, he accepted that he was as responsible for the state of affairs in Jerusalem as if he was there himself.

Intercession is not done from a position of superiority but from a place of empathy. It is standing in the gap, speaking on behalf of someone else. Maybe we will get better results in intercession as we adopt the heart posture Nehemiah displays

"But the LORD was pleased to crush Him, putting Him to grief; If He would render Himself as a guilt offering, He will see His offspring, He will prolong His days, And the good pleasure of the LORD will prosper in His hand."
-Isaiah 53:10 (NASB)

"In the same way, the Spirit helps us in our weakness. We do not know what we ought to pray for, but the Spirit himself intercedes for us through wordless groans."
-Romans 8:26

"For we do not have a high priest who is unable to empathize with our weaknesses, but we have one who has been tempted in every way, just as we are—yet he did not sin."
-Hebrews 4:15

— Word of the Day —
PASSION

Is defined as a strong liking or desire for or devotion to some activity, object, or concept[3]. What am I passionate about? The things that touch my emotions, the activities I would spend time and energy on without any noticeable reward, are clues to what God wants me to do. Passion is a necessary ingredient in life. Make room for things that touch your passion even if it isn't your day job.

— What is God saying to me now? —

What are the things breaking my heart? What does God
want me to do about it?

. . . .

. . . .

. . . .

. . . .

. . . .

. . . .

. . . .

. . . .

. . . .

. . . .

. . . .

. . . .

. . . .

. . . .

. . . .

. . . .

. . . .

REMEMBER

"Remember the instruction you gave your servant Moses, saying, 'If you are unfaithful, I will scatter you among the nations, but if you return to me and obey my commands, then even if your exiled people are at the farthest horizon, I will gather them from there and bring them to the place I have chosen as a dwelling for my Name.'
"They are your servants and your people, whom you redeemed by your great strength and your mighty hand."
-Nehemiah 1:8-10

Do you ever have difficulty reconciling the immutability of God's Word with His mercy? He promised to scatter the Israelites if they were unfaithful, and He did. He also promised to gather them together if they repent. This did not seem to be happening, and Nehemiah now reminds God of His promise.

God means what He says and says what He means. There is punishment for sin and consequences for wrongdoing. There is mercy after repentance and restoration after loss. The Israelites sinned and were punished. They went through exile for the seventy years God had prescribed. In the course of time, Daniel and other people stood in the gap, and God gathered the people back to the Promised Land. The remnant had returned to Jerusalem, but alas, all was not well with them.

Nehemiah took the case to God. Like a fine lawyer, he laid out the arguments and reminded God of His Word. This is the part that always bothers me—why do we need to remind God? Did He forget His promises to me? I know God forgets my sins, but I would hope He remembers His Word to me. I wonder if the instruction to remind Him is more for us than for Him.

For us to remind Him, we must know what He said and believe He is willing and able to do it. This is what prayer is—us asking the Father to do His will and not ours. The Father's reputation is on the line, and since it is impossible for God to lie, we can be assured His Word will stand.

Daniel reminded God the people called by His name were in trouble: *"Now, our God, hear the prayers and petitions of your servant. For your sake, Lord, look with favor on your desolate sanctuary. Give ear, our God, and hear; open your eyes and see the desolation of the city that bears your Name. We do not make requests of you because we are righteous, but because of your great mercy. Lord, listen! Lord, forgive! Lord, hear and act! For your sake, my God, do not delay, because your city and your people bear your Name" (Daniel 9:17-19)*

Nehemiah reminded God that the people He had redeemed were in disgrace.

We do not offend God when we remind Him of His Word. We can always go to God boldly. If what you see is different from what God promised, then come boldly. There is mercy and grace there. He will listen and forgive! He will hear and act! He will not delay, because you bear His Name.

Come boldly.

"I, even I, am he who blots out your transgressions, for my own sake, and remembers your sins no more. Review the past for me, let us argue the matter together; state the case for your innocence."
-Isaiah 43:25-26

"Let us then approach God's throne of grace with confidence, so that we may receive mercy and find grace to help us in our time of need."
-Hebrews 4:16

"Because God wanted to make the unchanging nature of his purpose very clear to the heirs of what was promised, he confirmed it with an oath. God did this so that, by two unchangeable things in which it is impossible for God to lie, we who have fled to take hold of the hope set before us may be greatly encouraged." -Hebrews 6:17-18

——— Word of the Day ———

COVENANT

A pact, treaty, alliance, or agreement between two parties of equal or of unequal authority[4]. Jesus died and rose again, fulfilling the terms of the new covenant and giving me eternal access to His throne. When I accepted Him into my heart, I received a passport that allows me to come before the Father. I can take my concerns, my victories, my shame, and my confusion to the Father because we are in a covenant.

— What is God saying to me now? —

Is there anything I am afraid to bring to God in prayer?

....
....
....
....
....
....
....
....
....
....
....
....
....
....
....
....
....
....

CUPBEARER

"Lord, let your ear be attentive to the prayer of this your servant and to the prayer of your servants who delight in revering your name. Give your servant success today by granting him favor in the presence of this man." I was cupbearer to the king.
-Nehemiah 1:11

I wish I could crawl into Nehemiah's head and figure out what was going through his mind at this time. What gave him the confidence to think he could build the wall when all others had failed? What skills did he have that qualified him to undertake this task? Maybe we are looking at this all wrong. Maybe he didn't know he could do it. Maybe it started with a single thought—what if you went to help build the wall? What if he dismissed that thought, but it kept coming back until it became a conviction? What we do know is a cupbearer became a governor, a builder, a man of arms, a master strategist, and a great leader.

Cupbearer! It sounds like such an easy job until you think about it. Nehemiah had to taste anything the king would drink to ensure it wasn't poisoned. He was the last line of defense since the king literally trusted Nehemiah with his life. Nehemiah knew what it meant to literally lay down his life daily to pursue a goal. Nehemiah would have had various safeguards in place around the wine or water served to the king. The greatest motivation for doing his job well was if he failed, he would pay for it with his life. Talk about incentives to have the key to the wine vault with him at all times. He would have had to keep his staff happy to ensure he nor the king were not targeted with poison.

Nehemiah would have learned the importance of management and control. Nehemiah was in constant contact with the king, privy to restricted information. He would have seen the king in a foul mood and when he was happy. He would have been there when the king did things worthy of respect, and when he made wrong decisions. Nehemiah would have had to give advice when asked and bite his tongue when not. Nehemiah learned discretion in his duty as cupbearer. He learned leadership and decision making and politics from maintaining close proximity to the king.

He learned everything he needed to become this beacon of leadership as he gave wine to the king. Nehemiah did not disdain his role as unimportant; he used it as a stepping stone to learning. There was no way he would have known the opportunity to be governor would arise. He cultivated excellence without grasping for new positions. Modern wisdom teaches us to be deliberate about climbing the corporate ladder. Nehemiah did not let the lack of opportunity deter him from being the best and learning from the people around him. As the old saying goes: opportunity met preparation! He understood he was in a position of authority for the good of Jerusalem.

David learned to be king of Israel by tending sheep, fighting in the army, and by leading misfits. Joseph learned to be prime minister by leading Potiphar's house and managing a prison. Paul learned to be a missionary by being a Pharisee prosecuting Christians. Moses learned to lead the children of Israel as a prince in the house of Pharaoh and as a shepherd tending Jethro's sheep. Our training grounds rarely resemble the place God is taking us to. What you need to settle in your heart is this—your experiences today will help you with your future.

"And we know that in all things God works for the good of those who love him, who have been called according to his purpose."
-Romans 8:28

"Praise be to the LORD my Rock, who trains my hands for war, my fingers for battle."
-Psalm 144:1

"But Joseph said to them, 'Don't be afraid. Am I in the place of God? You intended to harm me, but God intended it for good to accomplish what is now being done, the saving of many lives.'"
-Genesis 50:19-20

── Word of the Day ──
TRANSFERABLE SKILLS

Abilities you can transfer from one job to another. Even if I am not currently doing what I would like to do in the future, what am I learning now that will help me succeed anywhere I go? Am I giving my best in my current job? I may not understand why I am where I am now, but I can rest assured God can use it to prepare me for where He is taking me to. My faithfulness in little will determine if I will have more.

— What is God saying to me now? —

What influence do you wield in your position that you
do not have the title for? How are you using your
training grounds?

....
....
....
....
....
....
....
....
....
....
....
....
....
....
....
....
....
....

What Do You Want?

*In the month of Nisan in the twentieth year of King Artaxerxes,
when wine was brought for him, I took the wine and gave it to the
king. I had not been sad in his presence before, so the king asked me,
"Why does your face look so sad when you are not ill? This can be
nothing but sadness of heart." I was very much afraid, but I said to
the king, "May the king live forever! Why should my face not look
sad when the city where my ancestors are buried lies in ruins, and
its gates have been destroyed by fire?" The king said to me, "What is
it you want?" Then I prayed to the God of heaven, and I answered
the king, "If it pleases the king and if your servant has found favor in
his sight, let him send me to the city in Judah where my ancestors
are buried so that I can rebuild it."*
-Nehemiah 2:1-5

If someone should give you a blank check today, what would you
write on it? I started thinking recently about what I would do if I was

given a million dollars, and I was not impressed with my answers. I realized I spend more time dreaming than taking steps to achieve those dreams.

Nehemiah had a burden for Jerusalem, and it was not a flash in the pan. His brother Hanani told him the state of Jerusalem in Kislev, which was the third month of the civil year. We know Nehemiah prayed and asked God to intervene, but here he was, four months later, in the month of Nisan with no progress. He probably started out hopeful, trusting that each morning would be the day he would talk to the king and get him to do something on behalf of Jerusalem. Day after day went by without results until finally, Nehemiah's discouragement was apparent on his face.

We don't really see the big deal in Nehemiah's sad countenance. But when you think about the supreme authority kings had in those times, we appreciate this was a life and death situation. In Esther's day, a person could be put to death for approaching the king if he didn't ask to see them. It's a far cry from how in the US, we call our senators and congressmen to make our voices heard because we "elected" them. King Artaxerxes could have taken personal affront to the fact that the privilege of being in his presence was not enough to keep his staff smiling.

We see Nehemiah got to where his passion for Jerusalem overrode his sixth sense of preserving his life. What are you willing to die for? What burns with so much passion in your heart that you are willing to give up security and significance for it? Here is a man who had become consumed with doing something about a problem, and he invested time into understanding how he would resolve it.

Nehemiah didn't just agonize about it, though; he had a vision for what he wanted to do about the problem. He saw the walls rebuilt! He saw Jerusalem safe! He saw the disgrace, trouble, and reproach rolled away. What interests me is Nehemiah most likely had never seen Jerusalem in all its glory. He was born in Babylon and learned about the glory of Jerusalem from the elders who had seen it. He had no frame of reference, but he had a vision of what was ahead. To fulfill his vision, Nehemiah would need to give up the comfort of Babylon and sacrifice the prestige of his job. He would put his life at risk! All for a city he had never seen.

Nehemiah was driven by his faith in the God of Israel: the God who promised He would restore Israel if they would repent and turn to Him. The vision to rebuild Jerusalem was birthed in the place of prayer. Nehemiah continued to dream of what God showed him, and that passion sustained him until the opportunity to act presented itself. He still didn't take things for granted but prayed and sought confirmation from God that this was the right opportunity to proceed. An already established relationship with God is required to confirm in your spirit that a direction is the way to go. Practicing hearing the voice of God in small things will always pay off when you need to hear God in the big things.

Nehemiah articulated what he wanted in very clear teams. It wasn't many words either—he wanted to rebuild Jerusalem. A vision that cannot be communicated is not likely to be achieved.

"And the LORD answered me, and said, Write the vision, and make it plain upon tables, that he may run that readeth it. For the vision is yet for an appointed time, but at the end it shall speak, and not lie: though it tarry, wait for it; because it will surely come, it will not tarry."
-Habakkuk 2:23 KJV

"Where there is no vision, the people perish: but he that keepeth the law, happy is he."
-Proverbs 29:18 KJV

"'For if you remain silent at this time, relief and deliverance for the Jews will arise from another place, but you and your father's family will perish. And who knows but that you have come to your royal position for such a time as this?' Then Esther sent this reply to Mordecai: 'Go, gather together all the Jews who are in Susa, and fast for me. Do not eat or drink for three days, night or day. I and my

attendants will fast as you do. When this is done, I will go to the king,
even though it is against the law. And if I perish, I perish.'"
  -Esther 4:14-16

—— Word of the Day ——
VISION

An experience in the life of a person, whereby a special revelation from God was received[5]. The ability to see something accomplished through the eyes of faith is what will sustain through growing pains and attacks from the enemy. A vision of the end will be an anchor through any storm. Like our Father, we must learn to see the end from the beginning.

— What is God saying to me now? —

Do you have something in your life that you are willing
to take a risk to accomplish? If you were to receive a
blank check now, what will you do with it?

....
....
....
....
....
....
....
....
....
....
....
....
....
....
....
....
....
....

. . . .
. . . .
. . . .
. . . .
. . . .
. . . .
. . . .
. . . .
. . . .
. . . .
. . . .
. . . .
. . . .
. . . .
. . . .
. . . .
. . . .
. . . .
. . . .
. . . .
. . . .
. . . .

THE GRACIOUS HAND OF GOD ON ME

Then the king, with the queen sitting beside him, asked me, "How long will your journey take, and when will you get back?" It pleased the king to send me; so I set a time. I also said to him, "If it pleases the king, may I have letters to the governors of Trans-Euphrates, so that they will provide me safe-conduct until I arrive in Judah? And may I have a letter to Asaph, keeper of the royal park, so he will give me timber to make beams for the gates of the citadel by the temple and for the city wall and for the residence I will occupy?" And because the gracious hand of my God was on me, the king granted my requests. So I went to the governors of Trans-Euphrates and gave them the king's letters. The king had also sent army officers and cavalry with me. When Sanballat the Horonite and Tobiah the Ammonite official heard about this, they were very much disturbed

that someone had come to promote the welfare of the Israelites.
-Nehemiah 2:6-10

I heard a story once that always challenges me about the difference between a wish and a plan. A motivational speaker was talking to a group and encouraging them to live their dreams. He asked a volunteer what he wished for, and the man's response was he wanted to own a Lamborghini. The speaker asked the man to come forward, close his eyes, and demonstrate to the audience how he would drive his Lamborghini when he gets it. The volunteer mimicked opening the door and getting in, and immediately the speaker stopped him and said, "You are not ready, you're not hungry!" The door of a Lamborghini opens upward, and this volunteer demonstrated the motions of a regular car opening sideways. He desired the car but had not spent the time to think through the reality of owning a Lamborghini.

Nehemiah went beyond having a vision for rebuilding Jerusalem. He had thought through the things he would need to get to Jerusalem. I can see him talking to his brother Hanani about wanting to go to Jerusalem and being told it would help to have a letter to the governors to guarantee his safety. He knew he would need timber and had researched the name of the person who could provide it. The level of forethought shows us Nehemiah not only prayed to God but also absolutely believed God would make a way for him to rebuild Jerusalem.

Nehemiah understood what it meant for the gracious hand of God to grant success to seemingly impossible dreams. We understand grace is God's unmerited favor, His supernatural ability on our ability. I think where we fail most is not giving grace anything to work on.

People typically fall in two camps—those who only do things they are fully capable of doing in their might and with readily available resources, and those who dare to dream of accomplishing the impossible. There is something to be said for always counting the cost of what you are trying to achieve. The key is what you do with that cost. Do you abandon your dreams because the cost is too high, or do you depend on the gracious hand of God to supply what you need?

Nehemiah received favor from the King and attributed this to the gracious hand of God. That favor meant provision and safety for Nehemiah. In later chapters, we will see Nehemiah encouraging people to build because of the gracious hand of God. For him, this guaranteed the project would be successful.

Ezra was a teacher of the law, a contemporary of Nehemiah. He also talked multiple times about the gracious hand of God! In Ezra 7:9, Ezra talks about arriving at his destination in four months. It can be inferred this journey took less time than expected. In Ezra 8, we hear his testimony of protection and of skilled resources assigned to building the temple attributed to the gracious hand of God.

What Nehemiah and Ezra knew was their accomplishments could not be done in their strength. The gracious hand of God was the determining factor between success and failure, and they returned the glory to the One who makes the impossible possible.

"I was ashamed to ask the king for soldiers and horsemen to protect us from enemies on the road, because we had told the king, 'The gracious hand of our God is on everyone who looks to him, but his great anger is against all who forsake him.'"
-Ezra 8:22

"But by the grace of God I am what I am, and his grace to me was not without effect. No, I worked harder than all of them—yet not I, but the grace of God that was with me."
-1 Corinthians15:10

"But he said to me, 'My grace is sufficient for you, for my power is made perfect in weakness.' Therefore I will boast all the more gladly about my weaknesses, so that Christ's power may rest on me."
-2 Corinthians 12:9

── Word of the Day ──

GRACE

The unmerited favor of God[6]. A prominent Old Testament word describing God's grace is *chesed*[7]. This word speaks of deliverance from enemies, affliction, or adversity. It also denotes enablement, daily guidance, forgiveness, and preservation.[8] This is the secret sauce that separates believers from the world. It's what some people call luck, but we know it is God's decision to bless the work of our hands.

— What is God saying to me now? —

Do you have projects and dreams you abandoned because you did not have the resources to handle them? Have you counted the cost, i.e., identified what you would need to accomplish this goal? Have you asked for God's gracious hand to supply all you need?

. . . .
. . . .
. . . .
. . . .
. . . .
. . . .
. . . .
. . . .
. . . .
. . . .
. . . .
. . . .
. . . .
. . . .

PROTECT YOUR DREAM

I went to Jerusalem, and after staying there three days I set out during the night with a few others. I had not told anyone what my God had put in my heart to do for Jerusalem. There were no mounts with me except the one I was riding on. By night I went out through the Valley Gate toward the Jackal Well and the Dung Gate, examining the walls of Jerusalem, which had been broken down, and its gates, which had been destroyed by fire. Then I moved on toward the Fountain Gate and the King's Pool, but there was not enough room for my mount to get through; so I went up the valley by night, examining the wall. Finally, I turned back and reentered through the Valley Gate. The officials did not know where I had gone or what I was doing, because as yet I had said nothing to the Jews or the priests or nobles or officials or any others who would be doing the work.

-Nehemiah 2:11-16

I find it interesting that Nehemiah did not tell the rest of the people what he wanted to do. He kept his dream close until he could verify the information he received from his brother and the rest of the people who had been to Jerusalem. Nehemiah displayed great wisdom in waiting to find out what the people were like and how they would respond to the seemingly impossible task of rebuilding in Jerusalem.

Nehemiah had good reason to be reticent about his plans. The children of Israel had real enemies who were invested in keeping them in trouble and disgrace. People who had great incentives to oppose the rebuilding of the walls were profiting from the state of Jerusalem. At this time, Nehemiah alone carried the vision, and attacking him would have truncated the vision prematurely.

God often gives us impossible dreams, and well-meaning people can try to talk us out of what God has told us to do. I know sometimes people need to be told that what they would like to do doesn't make sense. However, I am learning if something doesn't make sense, it does not mean it's not from God. It did not make sense for Mary to become the mother of Jesus. It did not make sense for Noah to build an ark.

I want to caveat that I don't believe we need to suspend reasoning because of a God-given dream. I believe people pursuing impossible dreams are aware their dream doesn't make sense but feel compelled by God to continue. This makes them more credible than people who seem to have lost touch with reality and would like to walk to the moon.

How many times do we truncate a vision because we talk too soon? How many times do we share what should still be sacred with people who would desecrate it? Joseph had a dream that he would become the leader over his father and brothers. I don't believe the issue was that the dream wasn't true. After all, we see it came to pass in the latter part of the Scriptures. I think Joseph's mistake was he spoke too soon, and he spoke to the wrong people. Now we know God can make everything work together for good, but I wonder how much pain Joseph would have avoided if he only spoke to the right people at the right time.

Another thing we see Nehemiah do is he took time to evaluate the condition of the walls and the gates before spreading the vision. He took the time to research or, as we say in business, performed "due diligence" to make sure he had his view of what the state of Jerusalem was. If we do not make a conscious effort to stay close to what God has committed in our hands, we risk becoming out of touch because we only get reports from third parties. Whether it is in managing a large organization or being a mother to your children, take the time to go to the source and evaluate for yourself the true condition of things. If God has put something in your hands, take the time to learn about it

"Suppose one of you wants to build a tower. Won't you first sit down and estimate the cost to see if you have enough money to complete it? For if you lay the foundation and are not able to finish it, everyone who sees it will ridicule you, saying, 'This person began to build and wasn't able to finish.'"
-Luke 14:28-30

"Then he went down to Nazareth with them and was obedient to them. But his mother treasured all these things in her heart."
-Luke 2:51

"Be sure you know the condition of your flocks, give careful attention to your herds; for riches do not endure forever, and a crown is not secure for all generations."
-Proverbs 27:23-24

"Now the Berean Jews were of more noble character than those in Thessalonica, for they received the message with great eagerness and examined the Scriptures every day to see if what Paul said was true."
-Acts 17:11

—— Word of the Day ——
DUE DILIGENCE

In every day English means doing your homework! If you are a dreamer, you may have "bright ideas" and blab to the whole world before the idea has had a chance to percolate. Do the work of researching what it would take to deliver your idea. A well thought out idea will have enough roots to withstand constructive criticism. A random thought will not survive the onslaught of logic.

— What is God saying to me now? —

Have you done any research on ideas God has given
you?

....
....
....
....
....
....
....
....
....
....
....
....
....
....
....
....
....
....

WORDS TO INSPIRE

Then I said to them, "You see the trouble we are in: Jerusalem lies in ruins, and its gates have been burned with fire. Come, let us rebuild the wall of Jerusalem, and we will no longer be in disgrace." I also told them about the gracious hand of my God on me and what the king had said to me. They replied, "Let us start rebuilding." So they began this good work. But when Sanballat the Horonite, Tobiah the Ammonite official and Geshem the Arab heard about it, they mocked and ridiculed us. "What is this you are doing?" they asked. "Are you rebelling against the king?" I answered them by saying, "The God of heaven will give us success. We his servants will start rebuilding, but as for you, you have no share in Jerusalem or any claim or historic right to it."
-Nehemiah 2:17-20

Nehemiah was a great communicator. He came from across the ocean to fulfill a dream. He had the resources the king gave to him.

He had examined the walls and gates of Jerusalem. He knew what had to be done, but he could not do it alone. Nehemiah needed the Israelites to see things could be different. He needed them to build. He followed a clear communication method to let the people know what was in his heart. He laid out the situation (you see the trouble we are in.) He recommended an action (let us rebuild the wall.) He painted a picture of the results we (will no longer be in disgrace.)

We have a lot to learn from how Nehemiah used this simple process to convince the people who had lived with the broken walls and burned gates for a period of time by painting a picture different from what they had been used to. Nehemiah pointed them to the evidence that God's blessing was upon him and the work. God is our Jehovah Jireh, and when He sends, He provides. Our problem is provision rarely looks like what we expect it to be. The ability to share a vision and align people to drive toward a common goal is the hallmark of a great leader. These people caught the vision, committed to the work, and began to build.

As expected at the beginning of every great work, a group of people arose who tried to kill the vision. Some people come with the best of intentions, thinking to save you from future heartbreak or financial insecurities. Some others are malicious, running down any ideas that do not originate from them. It may be a snide comment or a heart to heart. Whatever form it takes, realize your vision is vulnerable here and needs to be protected. Don't allow those who are not invested in your dream to kill it

Nehemiah rightly identified the motives of Sanballat, Tobias, and Gershem. They were not there to offer constructive criticism. They were there to mock the work and ridicule the people. These people did not have a relationship with God nor the promise of His help. They were right in thinking it was improbable the work would be successful. They had no frame of reference for the grace and power and blessing of God on a project or people.

God's job is to grant success. Our responsibility is to do the work. There is no space here for outsiders. We need to know people not invested in the work, people who have not caught the vision may ridicule. People make fun of what they do not understand or cannot do. People make fun of what they cannot claim credit for. We have to make up our minds to ignore any detractors who are not encouraging us to do the work God called us to do.

"So all the skilled workers who were doing all the work on the sanctuary left what they were doing and said to Moses, 'The people are bringing more than enough for doing the work the LORD commanded to be done.' Then Moses gave an order and they sent this word throughout the camp: 'No man or woman is to make anything else as an offering for the sanctuary.' And so the people

were restrained from bringing more, because what they already had was more than enough to do all the work."
 -Exodus 36:47

"The LORD said, 'If as one people speaking the same language they have begun to do this, then nothing they plan to do will be impossible for them.'"
 -Genesis 11:6

"Commit to the LORD whatever you do, and he will establish your plans."
 -Proverbs 16:3

— Word of the Day —
SHARED VISION

An end goal or objective that a leader and his or her team establish and work toward together[9]. When a vision can be communicated and caught by other people, it's on the way to fulfillment. People will do much more for something they believe in than for something they are simply paid for. As a leader, I must be able to communicate my vision until the right people share it. As a follower, I must be able to work toward the fulfillment of a shared vision as if it is my vision.

— What is God saying to me now? —

Are there dreams I have abandoned because of mockery and ridicule? What shared vision do I need to commit to?

....
....
....
....
....
....
....
....
....
....
....
....
....
....
....
....
....

FIRST
FRUITS

Eliashib the high priest and his fellow priests went to work and rebuilt the Sheep Gate. They dedicated it and set its doors in place, building as far as the Tower of the Hundred, which they dedicated, and as far as the Tower of Hananel. The men of Jericho built the adjoining section, and Zakkur son of Imri built next to them. The Fish Gate was rebuilt by the sons of Hassenaah. They laid its beams and put its doors and bolts and bars in place. Meremoth son of Uriah, the son of Hakkoz, repaired the next section. Next to him Meshullam son of Berekiah, the son of Meshezabel, made repairs, and next to him Zadok son of Baana also made repairs. The next section was repaired by the men of Tekoa, but their nobles would not put their shoulders to the work under their supervisors.
-Nehemiah 3:1-5

I love that the first record of anyone building the wall was of the high priest and his fellow priests. They not only led the way by building but also dedicated the Sheep Gate to God.

Some historical sources say the Sheep Gate was used to bring sheep that would be for sacrifice into the city and thus the temple. Eliashib built this first because it was important to him and to Nehemiah that the norms and traditions related to the worship of God should be the biggest priority. They put God before any other economic decisions, and then they dedicated it.

The wall needed to be complete before it would be effective. Dedicating the Sheep Gate feels a little premature, given they did not know if it would ever be completed. The exiles had been back in Jerusalem for years. There would have been multiple attempts to rebuild that failed or proved insurmountable for those who had tried. This was truly a group effort and needed to be done as one body.

But Eliashib decided to build in front of the temple and dedicate it to God. They also did not wait for all the other gates or parts of the walls to be built, but they lifted the Sheep Gate up onto God as a first fruit. Eliashib was sending a message to everyone that he was stepping out in faith, believing the gracious hand of God would do it. And God proved His faithfulness by making it possible for the work to be completed. Do you have the faith to give the first to God even when you do not know if you will complete it? This gate would be used only for God—to allow animals in to be sacrificed. Time after time, we see the importance of putting God first in everything we do.

I found the contrast between the leadership and faith of Eliashib with the nobles of Tekoa interesting. Eliashib worked with his fellow priests to build even though he was the high priest. On the other hand, the nobles of Tekoa refused to submit to the supervisors, believing themselves too important to stoop to manual labor. In the end, their pride led to obscurity. The nobles of Tekoa were more concerned about their agenda rather than God's agenda. The wall was built, but their names are not mentioned. They missed the chance to go down in history and instead became irrelevant.

In modern times, we are under pressure to be leaders and influencers—at least on social media. We can get so caught up with appearances that we forget what it means to humble ourselves and work. When doing God's will is the most important part of our lives, we will throw ourselves into it without looking for personal recognition. Indeed, part of being a good leader is experiencing being a good follower. Pride will ultimately destroy any man because "God opposes the proud but shows favor to the humble"" (James 4:6).

"Honor the Lord with your wealth, with the firstfruits of all your crops; then your barns will be filled to overflowing, and your vats will brim over with new wine."
-Proverbs 3:9-10

"Humble yourselves, therefore, under God's mighty hand, that he

may lift you up in due time."
 -1 Peter 5:6

"Jesus called them together and said, 'You know that the rulers of the Gentiles lord it over them, and their high officials exercise authority over them. Not so with you. Instead, whoever wants to become great among you must be your servant, and whoever wants to be first must be your slave—just as the Son of Man did not come to be served, but to serve, and to give his life as a ransom for many.'"
 -Matthew 20:25-28

"Commit to the Lord whatever you do, and he will establish your plans."
 -Proverbs 16:3

—— Word of the Day ——
PRIORITIES

It is the most important thing you have to do or deal with, or must be done and death with before everything else you have to do[10]. My priorities will determine what I pay attention to, what I insist must be done, and where I direct my scarce resources. When God is my priority, I honor Him first in everything else I do. Pleasing Him drives my actions even if I do not get glory out of it.

— What is God saying to me now? —

Am I putting God first in everything I do?

....
....
....
....
....
....
....
....
....
....
....
....
....
....
....
....
....
....
....

ONE BITE
AT A TIME

The Jeshanah Gate was repaired by Joiada son of Paseah and
Meshullam son of Besodeiah. They laid its beams and put its doors
with their bolts and bars in place. Next to them, repairs were made
by men from Gibeon and Mizpah—Melatiah of Gibeon and Jadon of
Meronoth—places under the authority of the governor of Trans-
Euphrates. Uzziel son of Harhaiah, one of the goldsmiths, repaired
the next section; and Hananiah, one of the perfume-makers, made
repairs next to that. They restored Jerusalem as far as the Broad
Wall. Rephaiah son of Hur, ruler of a half-district of Jerusalem,
repaired the next section. Adjoining this, Jedaiah son of Harumaph
made repairs opposite his house, and Hattush son of Hashabneiah
made repairs next to him.
-Nehemiah 3:6-10

I was taking a walk in the neighborhood once and came across a
beautiful gate that immediately caught my attention. It seemed this

gate was purely for decorative purposes since it was freestanding i.e. not attached to a fence. While a car could not get through, any one on foot could walk around the gate to get into the property or maybe open the gate. In my opinion, a gate is useless if it is not attached to a wall. A wall is useless if the space for the gate is left open.

Imagine my surprise when I found out an ancient kingdom had this kind of wall built. History tells us in early civilization, 2047-1750 BCE, King Shulgi of the Sumerian city of Ur constructed a wall 155 miles (250 kilometers) long specifically to keep the Amorites out of Sumer. The wall was too long to be properly manned, however, and also presented the problem of not being anchored at either end to any kind of obstacle. An invading force could simply walk around the wall to bypass it, and that seems to be precisely what the Amorites did[11].

The children of Israel knew every piece of the wall had to connect and all the gates had to be built before this would be a useful exercise. They committed to build as one body. It didn't matter what their original jobs were, every one became a wall builder. Hananiah was a perfume maker, Uzziel was a goldsmith. Even when their primary skills were not required for the job at hand, they built. How many times do we insist on doing what we want to or are used to doing, rather than what needs to be done? If these men insisted on making gold and perfume, they would not be noted as part of the miracle which was the wall.

Remember the old saying: how do you eat an elephant—one bite at a time. Rebuilding the wall was an insurmountable task until it was broken down into bite sized chunks. With each person contributing, the work of restoring the walls became a doable task. Some repaired in front of their houses. Some handled gates. Everyone was working toward a common goal. They might not have seen the full picture and connectedness of the wall, but they were united in their purpose. They knew each person doing their part for the common good was what they needed to succeed.

The Bible tells us about the people settled in Shinar and decided to build a city with a high tower. To build something this large, they would need to have a lot of stone and mortar. I imagine these materials were scarce and would have made the goal difficult to achieve. They worked together to innovate, discovering they could bake bricks to replace stone and use tar rather than mortar. Working together, they developed enough wisdom to build a city and make an edifice for themselves. God looked at the work and declared their united front was all they needed to accomplish anything. When people are united in purpose, they can accomplish anything they set their hearts to.

"Now the whole world had one language and a common speech. As people moved eastward, they found a plain in Shinar and settled there. They said to each other, 'Come, let's make bricks and bake

them thoroughly.' They used brick instead of stone, and tar for mortar. Then they said, 'Come, let us build ourselves a city, with a tower that reaches to the heavens, so that we may make a name for ourselves; otherwise we will be scattered over the face of the whole earth.' But the LORD came down to see the city and the tower the people were building. The LORD said, 'If as one people speaking the same language they have begun to do this, then nothing they plan to do will be impossible for them.'"
-Genesis 11:16

"Again, truly I tell you that if two of you on earth agree about anything they ask for, it will be done for them by my Father in heaven."
-Matthew 18:19

"He replied, 'Because you have so little faith. Truly I tell you, if you have faith as small as a mustard seed, you can say to this mountain, "Move from here to there," and it will move. Nothing will be impossible for you.'"
-Matthew 17:20

—— Word of the Day ——
UNITY

Oneness of sentiment, affection or behavior[12]. Unity is not the same thing as uniformity which is an outward expression. Unity is a heart decision that plays out in what we do rather than how we look. It's important to celebrate the differences in people while encouraging unity of purpose in achieving our goals.

— What is God saying to me now? —

Am I closing my heart to opportunities because they
are not in my comfort zone? Is there a lack of unity in
anything I am a part of?

. . . .

. . . .

. . . .

. . . .

. . . .

. . . .

. . . .

. . . .

. . . .

. . . .

. . . .

. . . .

. . . .

. . . .

. . . .

. . . .

. . . .

ALL HANDS ON DECK

*Malkijah son of Harim and Hasshub son of Pahath-Moab repaired
another section and the Tower of the Ovens. Shallum son of
Hallohesh, ruler of a half-district of Jerusalem, repaired the next
section with the help of his daughters. The Valley Gate was repaired
by Hanun and the residents of Zanoah. They rebuilt it and put its
doors with their bolts and bars in place. They also repaired a
thousand cubits of the wall as far as the Dung Gate. The Dung Gate
was repaired by Malkijah son of Rekab, ruler of the district of Beth
Hakkerem. He rebuilt it and put its doors with their bolts and bars
in place. The Fountain Gate was repaired by Shallun son of Kol-
Hozeh, ruler of the district of Mizpah. He rebuilt it, roofing it over
and putting its doors and bolts and bars in place. He also repaired
the wall of the Pool of Siloam, by the King's Garden, as far as the
steps going down from the City of David. Beyond him, Nehemiah
son of Azbuk, ruler of a half-district of Beth Zur, made repairs up to*

a point opposite the tombs of David, as far as the artificial pool and
the House of the Heroes.
-Nehemiah 3:11-16

In the middle of reporting on the state of affairs for rebuilding the wall, Nehemiah includes a special mention of Shallum and how he repaired the wall with the help of his daughters. I have found that whenever the Bible stops to mention a woman's accomplishment, it is because she has stepped out of the ordinary and done what should have been impossible in a misogynistic society.

We hear of Abigail, whose wisdom stopped David from avenging himself over Nabal in anger. We hear of Ruth, whose sacrifice to care for her mother-in-law eventually led to her being included in the lineage of Jesus. We know about Esther, who was prepared to die in the bid to save the children of Israel. There is Deborah, the prophetess who was at the forefront as the people went to war. Interspersed through the Bible are stories that show us that in a time where the daughters were rarely recorded in genealogy, God was mindful of the women.

Perhaps the strongest example for me personally is the daughters of Zelophehad who forever changed the laws regarding inheritance in Israel. These women went to Moses and challenged the practice of giving the inheritance of a man who died without daughters to his closest male relative. Give us property among our father's relatives they said. The beauty of this story is God supported them and they became the first women to have an inheritance given directly to them and not their husbands.

I see the daughters of Shallum breaking stereotypes like their female ancestors. Why would their father not have help simply because he had no sons? Even in our day and time, wall building is still widely classified as men's work. The strength involved and the manual nature of the work discourages many women from embracing this type of work. However, Shallum's daughters did not let the labor or any form of ridicule stop them from rebuilding. We have no record that the other residents Shallum ruled over contributed to rebuilding. Maybe they did not catch the vision or believe it was worthwhile to rebuild. Maybe they would wait to see where this effort led before joining in. But thank God Shallum had his daughters.

Sometimes, help comes from an unexpected source. Sometimes it's the people who are least qualified, or still rough around the edges who develop into David's mighty men. We need to get to where we understand that when God gives us provision, it doesn't always look like what we expect. Moses' staff can split the Red Sea. A little boy's lunch can feed five thousand. David's rabble can become mighty men. Joseph's suffering can deliver Israel from famine. Don't look down on what God has given you. Ask Him to show you what you can do with what is in your hands.

"The daughters of Zelophehad son of Hepher, the son of Gilead, the son of Makir, the son of Manasseh, belonged to the clans of Manasseh son of Joseph. The names of the daughters were Mahlah, Noah, Hoglah, Milkah and Tirzah. They came forward and stood before Moses, Eleazar the priest, the leaders and the whole assembly at the entrance to the tent of meeting and said, 'Our father died in the wilderness. He was not among Korah's followers, who banded together against the Lord, but he died for his own sin and left no sons. Why should our father's name disappear from his clan because he had no son? Give us property among our father's relatives'... 'What Zelophehad's daughters are saying is right. You must certainly give them property as an inheritance among their father's relatives and give their father's inheritance to them.'"
  -Numbers 27:1-4, 7

"Then the LORD said to him, 'What is that in your hand?' 'A staff,' he replied. The LORD said, 'Throw it on the ground.' Moses threw it on the ground and it became a snake, and he ran from it. Then the LORD said to him, 'Reach out your hand and take it by the tail.' So Moses reached out and took hold of the snake and it turned back into a staff in his hand. 'This,' said the Lord, 'is so that they may believe that the LORD, the God of their fathers—the God of Abraham, the God of Isaac and the God of Jacob—has appeared to you.'"
  -Exodus 4:25

"'We have here only five loaves of bread and two fish,' they answered. 'Bring them here to me,' he said... They all ate and were satisfied, and the disciples picked up twelve basketfuls of broken pieces that were left over. The number of those who ate was about five thousand men, besides women and children."
-*Matthew 14:17-18, 20-21*

──── **Word of the Day** ────
INCLUSION

The act of including someone or something as part of a group[13]. Inclusion does not happen naturally. It's a deliberate effort to make people who do not look like you a part of your life. People naturally form cliques and may not notice someone is excluded. Beyond the emotion is the danger of excluding people from opportunities because they are not the stereotype. We must understand talent can be hidden and be open to the unexpected

— What is God saying to me now? —

Is my circle diverse enough? Am I inclusive in my relationships with others?

....
....
....
....
....
....
....
....
....
....
....
....
....
....
....
....
....

. . . .
. . . .
. . . .
. . . .
. . . .
. . . .
. . . .
. . . .
. . . .
. . . .
. . . .
. . . .
. . . .
. . . .
. . . .
. . . .
. . . .
. . . .
. . . .
. . . .
. . . .
. . . .

THE ZEALOUS ONE

Next to him, the repairs were made by the Levites under Rehum son of Bani. Beside him, Hashabiah, ruler of half the district of Keilah, carried out repairs for his district. Next to him, the repairs were made by their fellow Levites under Binnu son of Henadad, ruler of the other half-district of Keilah. Next to him, Ezer son of Jeshua, ruler of Mizpah, repaired another section, from a point facing the ascent to the armory as far as the angle of the wall. Next to him, Baruch son of Zabbai zealously repaired another section, from the angle to the entrance of the house of Eliashib the high priest. Next to him, Meremoth son of Uriah, the son of Hakkoz, repaired another section, from the entrance of Eliashib's house to the end of it. The repairs next to him were made by the priests from the surrounding region. Beyond them, Benjamin and Hasshub made repairs in front of their house; and next to them, Azariah son of Maaseiah, the son of Ananiah, made repairs beside his house.

-Nehemiah 3:17-23

One thing Nehemiah was really good at was providing commentary to what would have been a very humdrum record of the people involved in the rebuilding of the wall. Hashabiah carried out repairs. Binnui carried out repairs. Ezer carried out repairs.

Then we come to Baruch and Nehemiah records a difference—Baruch zealously repaired his section. What did Baruch do differently? What made Nehemiah notice Baruch! How do you repair a wall zealously? Do you work longer hours than the others? Do you arrange the stones meticulously? Do you sing and dance while repairing or is this about talking to other people to encourage them to build? We don't know the exact actions that caused Baruch to stand out so this is wide open for us to draw our own conclusions. Going beyond the actions Nehemiah saw, I also wonder what was responsible for Baruch's zeal. Maybe we should take a step back and understand what zeal is all about!

I checked other translations to see how they interpreted Baruch's actions. Some translations used different words instead of zeal—eagerly (CEV), diligently (CSB), earnestly (ASV), thoroughly (CEB), or carefully repaired (NKJV). The King James dictionary defines ZEAL as "passionate ardor in the pursuit of any thing. In general, zeal is an eagerness of desire to accomplish or obtain some object, and it may be manifested either in favor of any person or thing, or in opposition to it, and in a good or bad cause."[14]

Zeal is an eagerness of desire and it's manifested in favor of something or someone. Zeal is birthed in the heart and visible in actions. Baruch may have been one of the exiles who returned to Jerusalem to rebuild the temple at Cyrus's decree. Like Nehemiah, he would have grown up listening to stories about the beauty of Jerusalem and the splendor of the walls. Then he returned to find a land devastated by war and overrun with danger. Day after day, he would have waited for things to get better and looked for a restoration of the Jerusalem of his dreams. Now here comes Nehemiah with a vision to rebuild the wall and Baruch could finally see his vision one step closer to reality. I believe his zeal came from this passion to see Jerusalem rebuilt and was revealed in his repairing the fence.

Bringing this home, I ask myself, what reveals my zeal? Zeal is not revealed in just what I talk about but in what I do! If someone should look at my life now, what would they see I am passionate about? Baruch did not simply like repairing fences, he was passionate about restoring Jerusalem and that's what led him to carefully repair the fences.

I see you there saying you are passionate about cooking. That's what you do earnestly or carefully. But why do you love cooking? Do you love it because it brings family close? Is this done because you are passionate about making sure no one stays hungry? Don't stop until you find the why behind your zeal! Zeal without knowledge is dangerous as you expend energy in the wrong direction. The zeal Saul had in the defense of the Torah is the same zeal that drove him to evangelize the world and write two thirds of the New Testament!

"For I can testify about them that they are zealous for God, but their zeal is not based on knowledge."
-Romans 10:2

"Whatever you do, work at it with all your heart, as working for the Lord, not for human masters, since you know that you will receive an inheritance from the Lord as a reward. It is the Lord Christ you are serving."
-Colossians 3:23-24

"Diligent hands will rule, but laziness ends in forced labor."
-Proverbs 12:24

"The men in charge of the work were diligent, and the repairs progressed under them. They rebuilt the temple of God according to its original design and reinforced it."
-2 Chronicles 24:13

──Word of the Day──
ATTITUDE

A position determined or taken to serve a purpose; a manner of acting, feeling or thinking that shows one's disposition, beliefs, opinions, etc.[15] My attitude to work should show I am a person of faith. The quality of my work, the diligence I demonstrate are an offshoot of my relationship with God.

— What is God saying to me now? —

What does my attitude to work say about my faith? Do
people see God in the way I work?

....

....

....

....

....

....

....

....

....

....

....

....

....

....

....

....

....

....

GETTING THINGS DONE

Next to him, Binnui son of Henadad repaired another section, from Azariah's house to the angle and the corner, and Palal son of Uzai worked opposite the angle and the tower projecting from the upper palace near the court of the guard. Next to him, Pedaiah son of Parosh and the temple servants living on the hill of Ophel made repairs up to a point opposite the Water Gate toward the east and the projecting tower. Next to them, the men of Tekoa repaired another section, from the great projecting tower to the wall of Ophel. Above the Horse Gate, the priests made repairs, each in front of his own house. Next to them, Zadok son of Immer made repairs opposite his house. Next to him, Shemaiah son of Shekaniah, the guard at the East Gate, made repairs. Next to him, Hananiah son of Shelemiah, and Hanun, the sixth son of Zalaph, repaired another section. Next to them, Meshullam son of Berekiah made repairs opposite his living quarters. Next to him, Malkijah, one of the

goldsmiths, made repairs as far as the house of the temple servants and the merchants, opposite the Inspection Gate, and as far as the room above the corner; and between the room above the corner and the Sheep Gate the goldsmiths and merchants made repairs.
  -Nehemiah 3:24-32

One of the most important lessons we learn from Nehemiah is that of actually having a plan to accomplish a goal. Throughout the third chapter of this book, we have read the account of how leader after leader had a portion of the wall to repair. As much as we know that no one was forced to participate in rebuilding the wall, we see an organized plan for what they needed to do.

There was also a careful record of who was doing what. I think Nehemiah would have learned this from prior work experience as the cupbearer to the king. He would've had to maintain control of everywhere the king's drink could go through to ensure the king was not poisoned on his watch. He now transferred that level of detail to the work of building the wall.

You may challenge my assertion that Nehemiah had a plan. I think the evidence is clear because he could tell us, thousands of years later, who led the repairs of each section of the wall. He did not leave it to chance that all the sections would eventually be repaired. We see some leaders repairing the walls outside their houses while others tackled the gates—all individual parts to achieve a lofty goal.

I am a firm believer in a maxim commonly attributed to Peter Drucker, "You cannot manage what you do not measure." While we may dither on what qualifies as the appropriate level of measurement and its related benefits, I hope we can agree that expecting everything to work itself out is a recipe for disaster in a project of this magnitude.

There is a school of thought that putting plans in place is a lack of faith because of the belief that God's hand on anything makes it successful. The presence of faith should not negate the presence of planning. We know God does not always show us the entirety of what He wants us to do. For the pieces He has shown us though, we need to turn that vision into actionable steps to achieve these because vision without direction will only breed frustration.

Nehemiah had a dream to rebuild the walls of Jerusalem. He had a vision that seemed impossible but faith that it was possible. That faith propelled him to work with the nobles and allocate sections until there was someone assigned to every section of the wall. And then Nehemiah managed the work—he saw the nobles who didn't work, he saw the daughters who broke convention, he saw the zealous builders, and he saw the ones who put God first!

"'Consider now, for the LORD has chosen you to build a house as the sanctuary. Be strong and do the work.' Then David gave his son Solomon the plans for the portico of the temple, its buildings, its storerooms, its upper parts, its inner rooms and the place of atonement. He gave him the plans of all that the Spirit had put in his mind for the courts of the temple of the LORD and all the surrounding rooms, for the treasuries of the temple of God and for the treasuries for the dedicated things. He gave him instructions for the divisions of the priests and Levites, and for all the work of serving in the temple of the LORD, as well as for all the articles to be used in its service."

-1 Chronicles 28:10-13

"The plans of the diligent lead to profit as surely as haste leads to poverty."

-Proverbs 21:5

"Commit to the LORD whatever you do, and he will establish your plans."

-Proverbs 16:3

—— Word of the Day ——

ORGANIZATION

An efficient and orderly approach to tasks.[16] This refers to carrying out your plans. Good organization allows proper allocation of resources and measurable success. Putting structure around tasks always makes it more manageable. Small projects can succeed with little organization, but structure and process become critical to success the larger the project is. Even if this is not a talent you have, it's a talent you hire and empower for fulfillment of your goals.

— What is God saying to me now? —

What do I need to get organized about? Where am I
lacking structure?

....
....
....
....
....
....
....
....
....
....
....
....
....
....
....
....
....
....
....

STICKS AND STONES

When Sanballat heard that we were rebuilding the wall, he became angry and was greatly incensed. He ridiculed the Jews, and in the presence of his associates and the army of Samaria, he said, "What are those feeble Jews doing? Will they restore their wall? Will they offer sacrifices? Will they finish in a day? Can they bring the stones back to life from those heaps of rubble—burned as they are?" Tobiah the Ammonite, who was at his side, said, "What they are building—even a fox climbing up on it would break down their wall of stones!" Hear us, our God, for we are despised. Turn their insults back on their own heads. Give them over as plunder in a land of captivity. Do not cover up their guilt or blot out their sins from your sight, for they have thrown insults in the face of the builders. So we rebuilt the wall till all of it reached half its height, for the people worked with all their heart.

-Nehemiah 4:1-6

A lot has been said about the veracity of the children's poem, "Sticks and Stones may break my bones but words will never harm me." One school of thought is led by a group seemingly impervious to what other people say about them. The other group of which I am one believes words leave deeper wounds than physical punishment. I think the difference in both groups is the speed at which they can reject non-affirming words and file them in the "not truth" column.

As a child, I preferred the physical pain of my mom taking a switch to me to the expressed disappointment of my father. An incident when I was ten taught me that I had to take control of who was allowed to speak into my life. I was preparing to take an optional exam and had to go to an "inner city" school to sit for it. Well, this center had widespread cheating and since I had recently become a Christian, I was determined not to participate. As I worked through a math question, the proctor looked over my shoulder and tried to tell me the answer. I shook my head to indicate I did not need his help, and he was so offended that he looked at me and said, "You will fail." I spent most of the rest of that exam trying to calm myself and eventually left in tears at the end. I went into my mother's arms and she comforted me. After a while, she went into an office to talk to the administrators and came back to inform me that I had scored the highest at that center. That tall young man in a black shirt in anger had pronounced words on me that had no basis in reality. I learned early to sift between constructive criticism and the destructive words of a bully.

Sanballat was the classic definition of a bully. He was a leader in Samaria who intended to keep the Israelites vulnerable and disgraced (Nehemiah 2:10). For a while, he held his peace, supposing Nehemiah would not accomplish much. However, this time the Israelites seemed to have their act together and the walls were going up. I found it interesting to study the types of things Sanballat ridiculed them on:

- ☒ **Their ability** – what are those feeble Jews doing! He was telling them they did not have what it takes to build the wall. The feeble can't build!
- ☒ **Their vision** – will they rebuild the wall! He was attacking the purpose and overall dream the Israelites had to have a city with walls.
- ☒ **Their faith** – will they offer sacrifices? He mocked their desire to worship God in peace.
- ☒ **Their plan**- will they finish in a day? He ridiculed their plans—the steps they had outlined to get the work done.
- ☒ **Their resources** - can they bring the stones back to life from those heaps of rubble—burned as they are? The Israelites did not have a lot of resources and had to sift through the rubble and reuse the burned stones.
- ☒ **Their work** - what they were building—even a fox climbing up on it would break down their stone wall! Tobias questioned the quality of their work saying it would not stand the test of time.

I know most of us have gone through ridicule of some sort. Sometimes you are told your dream is trash. Other times you are told you don't have what it takes to succeed. Ridicule comes to belittle you and make you small. So the next time you are subject of ridicule, do what Nehemiah did—call on the God who fights for the despised and then build with all your heart!

"All her people groan as they search for bread; they barter their treasures for food to keep themselves alive. 'Look, LORD, and consider, for I am despised.'"
 -Lamentations 1:11

"God chose the lowly things of this world and the despised things—and the things that are not—to nullify the things that are, so that no one may boast before him."
 -1 Corinthians 1:28-29

"But we have this treasure in jars of clay to show that this all-surpassing power is from God and not from us. We are hard pressed on every side, but not crushed; perplexed, but not in despair; persecuted, but not abandoned; struck down, but not destroyed."
 -2 Corinthians 4:7-9

"But you, LORD, are a shield around me, my glory, the One who lifts my head high."
 -Psalm 3:3

──Word of the Day──

AFFIRMATION

The act of confirming something to be true.[17] We must speak the truth of God's Word to ourselves. The Word of God is full of truths we can use to combat the lies of the enemy. Chose to believe what God says about you. As a leader, you should also choose to affirm people around you. Let your words always be seasoned with salt! (Colossians 4:6).

— **What is God saying to me now?** —

Who am I allowing to speak into my life? Are there
words I need to move to the "not truth" column

....
....
....
....
....
....
....
....
....
....
....
....
....
....
....
....
....
....

IN TIMES OF ADVERSITY

But when Sanballat, Tobiah, the Arabs, the Ammonites and the people of Ashdod heard that the repairs to Jerusalem's walls had gone ahead and that the gaps were being closed, they were very angry. They all plotted together to come and fight against Jerusalem and stir up trouble against it. But we prayed to our God and posted a guard day and night to meet this threat. Meanwhile, the people in Judah said, "The strength of the laborers is giving out, and there is so much rubble that we cannot rebuild the wall." Also our enemies said, "Before they know it or see us, we will be right there among them and will kill them and put an end to the work."
Then the Jews who lived near them came and told us ten times over, "Wherever you turn, they will attack us." Therefore I stationed some of the people behind the lowest points of the wall at the exposed places, posting them by families, with their swords, spears and bows.
 -Nehemiah 4:7-13

The situation with Sanballat and the other tribes' opposition was not getting better. These men had progressed from ridicule and now intended to attack Jerusalem to stop the work. I wonder what Sanballat had to gain. Did he profit economically from keeping them vulnerable? Did it make him feel more powerful or superior to the Israelites? We may never know the full picture of why these people opposed the wall in Jerusalem. What we can be certain of is God is on the side of the downtrodden, and He will lift up those who are oppressed.

The Israelites were now facing trouble from every side and their enemies were united against them. The honeymoon phase was over, and now there would be real consequences for rebuilding the wall. This is the point where dreams fail and projects cease—the point of adversity. This is the point where your strength comes into play for *"If you falter in a time of trouble, how small is your strength!"* *(Proverbs 24:10).*

I think we have a lot to learn from how Nehemiah responded to this threat. Nehemiah did not ignore the threat. There is a school of thought that once God calls you to do something, everything will work out easily. Over and over in Scripture, we see people doing God's work face opposition. Our hope comes from their triumph in the end. Faith is not blind; it just puts things in the perspective of God's Word. Nehemiah went first to God in prayer, and this is what drove his actions.

His response was also commensurate to the threat. He started with posting guards to alert them to any trouble and as additional intelligence came, graduated to having the people themselves guarding the wall. The plot of their enemies failed on all levels—the element of surprise was lost because the Israelites were informed. The tactic of stealth was abandoned because the people were vigilant. The search for weak spots was futile because the perimeter was all round secure.

It's interesting the reason they were building the wall was to prevent these things from happening in the first place. In a city with walls, they would go in and defend from behind the safety of the wall. Now they had to put people at the lowest points because this is where they were exposed. They even had to stop building and start guarding the wall full time. This time however, the Israelites were invested in the wall and willing to fight for it.

Another thing to note was Nehemiah kept the lines of communication with the Jews who lived near the Samaritans open. They came ten times and told them what was being planned. Nehemiah didn't discourage them from bringing him "bad news." He listened to what they had to say and acted on it. In truth, if they had not been able get to Nehemiah, they would have gone to the people directly and caused worse trouble in discouraging them.

The biggest challenge they faced at this time was the enemy within. The strength of the laborers was giving out. They were facing a reality check and beginning to see that building a wall was not as easy as it seemed.

People start new projects with enthusiasm until you literarily hit a wall. Sometimes that wall is fatigue. Other times it is discouragement or opposition or fear. No worthwhile venture occurs without some resistance. Your ability to move beyond this is the difference between success and failure. The trick to this though is to win the battle first in your mind!

"The thief comes only to steal and kill and destroy; I have come that they may have life, and have it to the full."
-John 10:10

"For everyone born of God overcomes the world. This is the victory that has overcome the world, even our faith."
-1 John 5:4

"God is our refuge and strength, an ever-present help in trouble."
-Psalm 46:1

──── **Word of the Day** ────

RESILIENCE

An ability to recover from or adjust easily to adversity or change.[18] Resilience is about toughness. It is being able to withstand anything thrown at you. It's about surviving in non-conducive environments. It's about finding strength in God to face any opposition. God is the anchor that holds us even when we are oppressed on every side. We can find strength in God to face any difficulty in life.

— What is God saying to me now? —

Have I given up on anything God gave me because of adversity?

....
....
....
....
....
....
....
....
....
....
....
....
....
....
....
....
....
....

DAY SEVENTEEN

EN GARDE

After I looked things over, I stood up and said to the nobles, the officials and the rest of the people, "Don't be afraid of them. Remember the Lord, who is great and awesome, and fight for your families, your sons and your daughters, your wives and your homes." When our enemies heard that we were aware of their plot and that God had frustrated it, we all returned to the wall, each to our own work. From that day on, half of my men did the work, while the other half were equipped with spears, shields, bows and armor. The officers posted themselves behind all the people of Judah who were building the wall. Those who carried materials did their work with one hand and held a weapon in the other, and each of the builders wore his sword at his side as he worked.
-Nehemiah 4:14-18a

Again we see Nehemiah didn't just speak. The report had come that the laborers' strength was going out. Nehemiah took time to assess the situation, prayed, and put practical steps in place to protect the people. Then he spoke to the people and asked them to fight.

We must remind ourselves this would be a matter of life and death. The easier solution would have been for the people to surrender and stop building the wall. After all, they had lived without the wall for some years. The disgrace was not new; the trouble was familiar. They could settle for the oppression of the Samaritans. But Nehemiah said, "Don't be afraid of them!" Fear has held you back for too long. It's time to rise above the emotion holding you back be it pain, sorrow, rejection, or regret. Trouble and disgrace should not be allowed to stay. Opposition will come when you make a change, but you stand your ground and do not be afraid.

Remember the Lord! Look to the One who is greater and can help you overcome. Instead of thinking of all the things threatening you, think of the things God has done for you. Remember when He saved you from sin, from addiction, or from death. Remember when He healed you, met your needs, gave you a job, or a place to stay! Remember how He knows everything about you and loves you the same! Remember how He has helped you over and over again to rise above limitations, fear, trouble, disgrace, and anything that held you down. Remember your God who is great and awesome—and fight!

Fight—not just for you but for your families, for your future, for unborn generations depending on you. Don't stay in the familiar and continue to suffer through what has tormented you for years. Choose faith, remember the Lord, and fight for something bigger than yourself! Nehemiah showed them a reason to fight for change. Sometimes it's not enough to fight for yourself. You need to see the effort you are making has a lasting impact on generations to come.

Once the people were ready to fight, Nehemiah records the plans of their enemies had been frustrated. They did not even need to fight. But even after they saw the victory, they did not relax. This seems like a metaphor for how we need to live our lives.

It's like when fencing, the opponent calls out "en garde" to alert you that he is about to strike. When Jesus was on earth, He already put us on alert, telling us the devil intended to put us in great trouble and disgrace. So when we're starting something new or breaking out of old habits, we cannot let down our guard. Even when the battle you are aware of is over, be vigilant and watch out for the attack of the enemy. Listen to that nudge in your spirit when God warns you not to do something. Watch over your family in prayer. Study the Word so you know and understand the times. Be diligent over your business. Trust in God's ability to protect you from the hand of the enemy! En garde!

"*Devote yourselves to prayer, being watchful and thankful.*"
  -Colossians 4:2

"*Be alert and of sober mind. Your enemy the devil prowls around like a roaring lion looking for someone to devour.*"
  -1 Peter 5:8

"*Do not forsake wisdom, and she will protect you; love her, and she will watch over you.*"
  -Proverbs 4:6

"*She watches over the affairs of her household and does not eat the bread of idleness.*"
  -Proverbs 31:27

"*For the LORD watches over the way of the righteous, but the way of the wicked leads to destruction.*"
  -Psalm 1:6

── Word of the Day ──
STRATEGY

A plan of action or policy designed to achieve a major or overall aim.[19] Different strategies are required for different situations. There is no magic bullet that resolves every situation. The strategy to win a battle is informed by the peculiarities of that situation and tailored to the environment. Take time to review the situation at hand and make creative solutions to achieve your goals.

— What is God saying to me now? —

Are there areas in my life where I have dropped my guard? Am I using the wrong strategies to fight my battles?

. . . .
. . . .
. . . .
. . . .
. . . .
. . . .
. . . .
. . . .
. . . .
. . . .
. . . .
. . . .
. . . .
. . . .
. . . .
. . . .

DAY EIGHTEEN

THE SOUND OF THE TRUMPET

But the man who sounded the trumpet stayed with me. Then I said to the nobles, the officials and the rest of the people, "The work is extensive and spread out, and we are widely separated from each other along the wall. Wherever you hear the sound of the trumpet, join us there. Our God will fight for us!" So we continued the work with half the men holding spears, from the first light of dawn till the stars came out. At that time I also said to the people, "Have every man and his helper stay inside Jerusalem at night, so they can serve us as guards by night and as workers by day." Neither I nor my brothers nor my men nor the guards with me took off our clothes; each had his weapon, even when he went for water.
-Nehemiah 4:18b-23

A few years ago, I was working on a project in Iowa and on the Wednesday afternoon at noon, a loud siren went off. My colleagues noticed my curious look and when I asked what the noise was, I was told it's a siren used to alert the community about tornados so they can take cover. It's tested at noon every Wednesday so if you hear it at any other time, you need to take shelter immediately.

This must have been the type of role that trumpets played in the time of Nehemiah. They couldn't send an alert to everyone's phone or announce on TV. Everyone had to listen for the sound of the trumpet. What I found even more interesting was that the man who sounded the trumpet stayed with Nehemiah. The people were already on high alert because of the threat of attack from their enemies. Apart from being armed for battle, one key to their survival would be their ability to band together and defend themselves. During this time, Nehemiah had a system to reach the people.

A few things jump out at me on how Nehemiah managed his communication amid a crisis. Probably most important was he was always prepared to communicate. Whether it was night or day, he had a method to get the information out to the people.

Now we know that having the trumpet close would have been useless if there was no way to get an early warning system for any section that would be attacked. There would have been a way for the sentry to reach him quickly so that he could alert the rest of the people using the trumpet. Communication must occur both ways—from the leader to the people and vice versa. Using a trumpet meant everyone could hear it. He did not speak to a limited few; he used a method where rich or poor, young or old could benefit from the information. The trumpet had to produce a definite sound the people were familiar with so that they knew what to do. The sound also birthed a clear action to gather at a central point and prepare to fight.

Perhaps the most important communication from Nehemiah came from what he did. By staying alert and always being armed and ready for battle, he showed he wasn't asking them for a sacrifice that he wasn't willing to make himself. We should never ask people to do what we are not willing to do ourselves. In taking up arms himself, Nehemiah was telling the people, we are in this together. I am willing to lay down my life to protect you; I will do everything in my power to keep you safe.

Nehemiah and his team went over and beyond what they asked the people to do. They did not relax, not in sleep, not to eat or drink. They kept watch over the people. Communication should be backed by action. Leaders don't just say, they do. Leaders don't just do, they do more. What we do is the highest form of communication.

"Even in the case of lifeless things that make sounds, such as the pipe or harp, how will anyone know what tune is being played unless there is a distinction in the notes? Again, if the trumpet does not sound a clear call, who will get ready for battle?"
-1 Corinthians 14:7-8

"The LORD says: 'These people come near to me with their mouth and honor me with their lips, but their hearts are far from me. Their worship of me is based on merely human rules they have been taught.'"
-Isaiah 29:13

"But in your hearts revere Christ as Lord. Always be prepared to give an answer to everyone who asks you to give the reason for the hope that you have. But do this with gentleness and respect."
-1 Peter 3:15

—— **Word of the Day** ——

TRANSPARENCY

Implies openness, communication, and accountability.[20] Transparency from a leader builds trust and confidence in his followers. The comfort of knowing a leader will communicate clearly and appropriately is key. Transparency ensures the leader can stay in contact with the people to understand the true priorities and concerns of the people.

— What is God saying to me now? —

Are my actions communicating the same things my
mouth is communicating?

....

....

....

....

....

....

....

....

....

....

....

....

....

....

....

....

....

....

STRICTLY BUSINESS

Now the men and their wives raised a great outcry against their fellow Jews. Some were saying, "We and our sons and daughters are numerous; in order for us to eat and stay alive, we must get grain." Others were saying, "We are mortgaging our fields, our vineyards and our homes to get grain during the famine." Still others were saying, "We have had to borrow money to pay the king's tax on our fields and vineyards. Although we are of the same flesh and blood as our fellow Jews and though our children are as good as theirs, yet we have to subject our sons and daughters to slavery. Some of our daughters have already been enslaved, but we are powerless, because our fields and our vineyards belong to others." When I heard their outcry and these charges, I was very angry. I pondered them in my mind and then accused the nobles and officials. I told them, "You are charging your own people interest!"
-Nehemiah 5:1-7a

The children of Israel were going through a trying time. They had been living vulnerable lives without a wall or gates in the city. Now that they were taking steps to protect themselves, their enemies were threatening to come and kill them suddenly. To compound the issue, a good number of them were facing an economic crisis and could not feed their families. Jerusalem was in crisis!

As at the time of writing this, the world is suffering through the COVID-19 pandemic. As a consequence of the unprecedented shutdown to slow the health crisis, some people cannot feed their families. Some will lose their home and businesses while others will go into debt. The world as we know it is in crisis. Yet, not everyone is suffering financially at this time. Some people's businesses are booming. Some are buying up businesses. In no time, people will buy up shares, houses, and cars that have to be given up by those who can no longer afford it. Like Winston Churchill said, "Never let a good crisis go to waste!"

The Jewish nobles and officials were businessmen. Their fellow Jews needed money and they could not pay. The nobles were not running a charity, so were they expected to give something for nothing? I could understand the outrage, but was this really justified? As a believer, the conundrum is when it crosses the line from being good business to taking advantage of people. How can you tell the difference so that you know when to draw the line?

I think we need to go back to the Bible to understand where the line is. Moses laid out the instructions from God on the social responsibility of the Israelites. They were to provide charity for those who could not afford to take care of themselves. They were to provide interest-free loans for those who needed some help to get back on their feet. The Scriptures were clear on affording the lender some dignity and ensuring these kinds of loans were not for profit.

There are various schools of thoughts on who was entitled to this kind of treatment. In the strictest sense, it was for the poorer Israelites only. Now that we are all brothers in Christ, some extend this to mean all believers. Without going into a theological lesson, we can agree to adopt the spirit of the instructions which is we should not take advantage of people!

Not only did the nobles disobey the law by charging interest, but they also took the collateral of their fellow Jews and impoverished them while they were in crisis. They did not see the evil in the fact people did not have enough to eat. Others were handing over their inheritance and source of livelihood just to afford to feed their families. Most heartbreaking was the people who sold their daughters to stay out of jail and put food on the table. All this because the nobles were doing "business."

So what does this mean for us as Christians? How do we balance the cost of doing business with the principles of fairness? How do you make sure people don't take advantage of you by obtaining loans they have no intention of returning? I think it comes from establishing the spirit of this law in how you operate your business or daily activities. Whether you are loaning someone money, wisdom, or time, in any circumstance when you are the lender, always treat your borrower with respect and dignity. Don't look to profit from someone else's misfortune but display compassion for people down on their luck. Be the hand of Jesus because wealth is given to you for a purpose.

"If you lend money to one of my people among you who is needy, do not treat it like a business deal; charge no interest. If you take your neighbor's cloak as a pledge, return it by sunset, because that cloak is the only covering your neighbor has. What else can they sleep in? When they cry out to me, I will hear, for I am compassionate."
-Exodus 22:25-27

"Do not take a pair of millstones—not even the upper one—as security for a debt, because that would be taking a person's livelihood as security."
-Deuteronomy 24:6

"The LORD detests dishonest scales, but accurate weights find favor with him."
-Proverbs 11:1

—— **Word of the Day** ——

COMPASSION

Sympathetic consciousness of others' distress together with a desire to alleviate it.[21] Compassion is needed in leadership to evaluate the impact of your decisions on other people. Compassion drives you to choices that may not always be the most profitable but will always have the best interest of people at heart.

— What is God saying to me now? —

Are there any business dealings I am involved in that
need to be infused with compassion?

....
....
....
....
....
....
....
....
....
....
....
....
....
....
....
....
....
....

WALKING IN THE FEAR OF THE LORD

So I called together a large meeting to deal with them and said: "As far as possible, we have bought back our fellow Jews who were sold to the Gentiles. Now you are selling your own people, only for them to be sold back to us!" They kept quiet, because they could find nothing to say. So I continued, "What you are doing is not right. Shouldn't you walk in the fear of our God to avoid the reproach of our Gentile enemies? I and my brothers and my men are also lending the people money and grain. But let us stop charging interest! Give back to them immediately their fields, vineyards, olive groves and houses, and also the interest you are charging them—one percent of the money, grain, new wine and olive oil." "We will give it back," they said. "And we will not demand anything more from them. We will do as you say." Then I summoned the priests and made the nobles and officials take an oath to do what they had promised. I also shook out the folds of my robe and said, "In this way may God shake out of their house and possessions anyone

who does not keep this promise. So may such a person be shaken out and emptied!" At this the whole assembly said, "Amen," and praised the Lord. And the people did as they had promised.
-Nehemiah 5:7b-13

Nehemiah called the nobles together to address the issue with charging interest from their fellow Jews. Their business practices had further impoverished the Jews by forcing them to mortgage their properties and enslave their children. It's important to pause and determine how they got to this point. The law explicitly said Jews should not charge interest from such loans. What had made them flout this law in the interest of making profit? It appears the nobles did not know or embrace the law.

In later chapters in Nehemiah, Ezra the priest read the law to the assembly, and they wept in sorrow when they realized they had been breaking the law. The nobles had adopted the business practices of the people around them and abandoned the principles commanded in God's Word. The Israelites—like us Christians—were required to live by a different standard, and they didn't even know what that standard was.

To do business God's way, we must know God's way. I think this is why God told the kings of Israel to always keep the scroll of the law with them. The king could only rule and execute judgment God's way if he studied God's directions. It's important to know what you stand for before pressure comes. It's wisdom to determine the principles you will live and work by so that your actions please God. This is not only talking about things that will get you in legal trouble. Hopefully, we all know to avoid those. It comes to play when the Word of God has a standard the world does not share. It goes to the heart of the reason behind your choices. Nehemiah refers to this as walking in the fear of God.

The Hebrew verb yare can mean "to fear, to respect, to reverence"[22] and the Hebrew noun *yirah* "usually refers to the fear of God and is viewed as a positive quality.[23]

The Greek noun *phobos* can mean "reverential fear" of God, "not a mere 'fear' of His power and righteous retribution, but a wholesome dread of displeasing Him.[24] The fear of the Lord is the beginning of wisdom. The wholesome dread of displeasing God is the wisdom you need to succeed in whatever you do.

The fear of the Lord teaches me that I cannot increase wealth at the expense of others and expect a blessing from God. It shows me that not all profit is good profit. The Bible doesn't tell us exactly who to deal with or how much of our income to give to charity or loan to the needy. I think God leaves that up to us to decide. What is important is that all your dealings do not go against the Word of God and where it is not cut and dry, we make choices that will please God. It also means that when you have done wrong, you repent and make every attempt to make it right. Continue to do right. Walk in the fear of God

"Better a little with the fear of the LORD than great wealth with turmoil."
-Proverbs 15:16

"Through love and faithfulness sin is atoned for; through the fear of the LORD evil is avoided."
-Proverbs 16:6

"All the people saw this and began to mutter, 'He has gone to be the guest of a sinner.' But Zacchaeus stood up and said to the Lord, 'Look, Lord! Here and now I give half of my possessions to the poor, and if I have cheated anybody out of anything, I will pay back four times the amount.' Jesus said to him, 'Today salvation has come to this house, because this man, too, is a son of Abraham. For the Son of Man came to seek and to save the lost.'"
-Luke 19:7-10

"Learn to do right; seek justice. Defend the oppressed. Take up the cause of the fatherless; plead the case of the widow."
-Isaiah 1:17

—— **Word of the Day** ——

INTEGRITY

Quality of being honest and having strong moral principles.[25] Integrity as they say is who you are when no one is looking. Integrity is also seen as uprightness, blamelessness, or sincerity. Our integrity is fed from the fear of God, that consciousness of God that regulates our actions even when there are no consequences to making certain decisions

— **What is God saying to me now?** —

Do I live with a consciousness of God in everything I
do?

. . . .

. . . .

. . . .

. . . .

. . . .

. . . .

. . . .

. . . .

. . . .

. . . .

. . . .

. . . .

. . . .

. . . .

. . . .

. . . .

. . . .

EXECUTIVE COMPENSATION

Moreover, from the twentieth year of King Artaxerxes, when I was appointed to be their governor in the land of Judah, until his thirty-second year—twelve years—neither I nor my brothers ate the food allotted to the governor. But the earlier governors—those preceding me—placed a heavy burden on the people and took forty shekels of silver from them in addition to food and wine. Their assistants also lorded it over the people. But out of reverence for God I did not act like that. Instead, I devoted myself to the work on this wall. All my men were assembled there for the work; we did not acquire any land. Furthermore, a hundred and fifty Jews and officials ate at my table, as well as those who came to us from the surrounding nations. Each day one ox, six choice sheep and some poultry were prepared for me, and every ten days an abundant supply of wine of all kinds. In spite of all this, I never demanded the food allotted to the governor, because the demands were heavy on these people.

Remember me with favor, my God, for all I have done for these people.
 -Nehemiah 5:14-19

Nehemiah provides a model for public office that is frankly a high bar to achieve. For the twelve years he was governor in Jerusalem, he refused to eat the food earmarked for the governor's use. To be clear, there would have been no sin if he had taken the food allotted to him. His decision to refuse this food was based on the impact this food tax was having on the people who were expected to provide it. These few verses provide a good insight into what motivated Nehemiah and guided his actions throughout his term as governor of Jerusalem.

Maybe the most important motivation for Nehemiah was a reverence for God. Reverence or alternatively the fear of God is what Nehemiah encouraged the nobles of Israel to have so that they would treat their fellow Jews right. The realization that we carry the name of the Lord should impact everything we do. It should be evident in our choices, our lifestyle, and in our dealings with the rich and poor alike.

We see the impact of the fear of the Lord in multiple things around Nehemiah. Not only did he refuse to burden the people with the food tax, but also his family also followed suit. We have no record that Nehemiah got married or had kids. This doesn't mean he did not, just that we don't know. Nehemiah talks about his brothers who filled leadership roles in Jerusalem. His brothers followed his example of putting the people first. We also look at his men. Prior servants may have lorded it over the people, but Nehemiah did not give his servants the authority to oppress the Jews or to enrich themselves. They were only to focus on the work. The way our family and staff behave is a reflection of the heart of the person who leads them. Nehemiah ruled with the fear of the Lord and this trickled down and was visible to all.

Another thing that was clear was Nehemiah's devotion to the work. The vision that drove him when he was still a cupbearer was in full effect. Nehemiah came to Jerusalem to build the wall. Becoming the governor was not his goal. Amassing a fortune was not his intention. He came to build a wall. We must constantly ask ourselves if we are still true to the heart of what God has called us to do. Does it have our full devotion? Is this what I expend my energy on? What holds my attention above everything else?

The last thing I would like to highlight is Nehemiah's concern for the people. Nehemiah displayed a shepherd's heart! The governor's ration was Nehemiah's legal right. However, he chose to forfeit it because of the impact on the people.

It boggles my mind that Nehemiah paid to feed 150 daily at his expense for twelve years. Where did he get the money from! It may have been his personal savings. It could be out of his salary as a governor. There may have been farmlands allotted to the king that his servants had to cultivate rather than tax the people. Whatever creative solution Nehemiah came up was at some personal cost to him! We won't all be able to feed 150 officials from our personal wealth. But we can all live with the principle that we will be mindful of what our rights are costing the people we serve.

"He has shown you, O mortal, what is good. And what does the LORD require of you? To act justly and to love mercy and to walk humbly with your God."
-Micah 6:8

"Son of man, prophesy against the shepherds of Israel; prophesy and say to them: 'This is what the Sovereign LORD says: Woe to you shepherds of Israel who only take care of yourselves! Should not shepherds take care of the flock?'"
-Ezekiel 34:2

"For I have chosen him, so that he will direct his children and his household after him to keep the way of the LORD by doing what is right and just, so that the LORD will bring about for Abraham what he has promised him."
-Genesis 18:19

——Word of the Day——
SACRIFICE

Giving up something valued for the sake of something else regarded as more important or worthy.[26] Leadership requires sacrifice as the focus needs to be on the greater good and not individual gain. There is no room for selfishness or greed in leadership. A leader must take care of his flock!

— **What is God saying to me now?** —

How do my actions and policies impact the people I am
serving? What can I do to make life easier for the
people I am responsible for?

. . . .

. . . .

. . . .

. . . .

. . . .

. . . .

. . . .

. . . .

. . . .

. . . .

. . . .

. . . .

. . . .

. . . .

. . . .

. . . .

. . . .

FINISHING STRONG

When word came to Sanballat, Tobiah, Geshem the Arab and the rest of our enemies that I had rebuilt the wall and not a gap was left in it—though up to that time I had not set the doors in the gates—Sanballat and Geshem sent me this message: "Come, let us meet together in one of the villages on the plain of Ono." But they were scheming to harm me; so I sent messengers to them with this reply: "I am carrying on a great project and cannot go down. Why should the work stop while I leave it and go down to you?" Four times they sent me the same message, and each time I gave them the same answer. Then, the fifth time, Sanballat sent his aide to me with the same message, and in his hand was an unsealed letter in which was written: "It is reported among the nations—and Geshem says it is true—that you and the Jews are plotting to revolt, and therefore you are building the wall. Moreover, according to these reports you are about to become their king and have even appointed prophets to

make this proclamation about you in Jerusalem: 'There is a king in Judah!' Now this report will get back to the king; so come, let us meet together." I sent him this reply: "Nothing like what you are saying is happening; you are just making it up out of your head." They were all trying to frighten us, thinking, "Their hands will get too weak for the work, and it will not be completed." But I prayed, "Now strengthen my hands."
-Nehemiah 6:1-9

The enemies of Israel seemed to follow a script they had used successfully in the past. In the book of Ezra when the Jews returned to rebuild the temple under Zerubbabel, their enemies conspired to stop them from building. They offered to join in building, but the Jews refused their help. They then discouraged the people, and when that didn't work, they tried to frighten them. After this, they bribed officials to make their life difficult. None of these shook the people. Finally, they wrote a letter to the new king and convinced him the Israelites were seditious and would revolt against the king. This time they were successful; the work on the temple was stopped, a delay that lasted about sixteen years. In time, the temple would be completed, but from start to finish, it had taken fifty-eight years.

Now Nehemiah had come in to lead the people in rebuilding the wall. Drawing from the same playbook, they had tried to sabotage the work but were unsuccessful. Intimidation, discouragement, and oppression did not yield results. The wall was up! The gaps were now closed and the end was in sight. All that was remaining was to put in the gates and the reproach of Israel would be at an end. Their enemies realized their opportunity to shut down this work was rapidly closing. All other tactics had failed. It was time to attack the leader! As stated in Zechariah 13:7, *"Strike the shepherd, and the sheep will be scattered."*

Nehemiah knew the invitation to meet in the plains of Ono was an elaborate plan to isolate him so that he could be imprisoned or even killed. He however did not accuse them of plotting to kill him. He gave a diplomatic response that is one of the most widely quoted verses in Nehemiah: "I am doing a great work, why should I leave that to consort with you" (v. 6:3). In the end, all the plots and intrigue boiled down to distractions. Because Nehemiah stayed focused on the end goal, he was not tempted to fraternize with others. He wasn't moved by flattery or curiosity. He concentrated on the work ahead of him.

Nehemiah also faced slander from his enemies. The open letter would be somewhat equivalent to posting a slanderous post on social media to force a response. If this report had reached the king, the work may have been stopped and Nehemiah recalled. However, Nehemiah had moved so fast on building the wall that there was no way to get to the king to stop the work before it was complete.

It didn't matter what was thrown at Nehemiah, his default response was always to ask for God's help. He asked God to strengthen his hands—to help him to do his work better, more effectively, to stand firm and not waver!

"Then the peoples around them set out to discourage the people of Judah and make them afraid to go on building. They bribed officials to work against them and frustrate their plans during the entire reign of Cyrus king of Persia and down to the reign of Darius king of Persia. At the beginning of the reign of Xerxes, they lodged an accusation against the people of Judah and Jerusalem."
-Ezra 4:4-6

"'Awake, sword, against my shepherd, against the man who is close to me!' declares the LORD Almighty. 'Strike the shepherd, and the sheep will be scattered, and I will turn my hand against the little ones.'"
-Zechariah 13:7

"Because the Sovereign LORD helps me, I will not be disgraced. Therefore have I set my face like flint, and I know I will not be put to shame."
-Isaiah 50:7

——— Word of the Day ———
FOCUS

Concentrating interest or activity on something.[27] During distractions, real or imagined, the leader must determine the key things that warrant his or her attention. Focus involves single-minded attention to delivering the vision. Every new activity or threat should be reviewed to evaluate its contribution to the ultimate goal.

— **What is God saying to me now?** —

Is there anything distracting me from my primary
mission?

. . . .

. . . .

. . . .

. . . .

. . . .

. . . .

. . . .

. . . .

. . . .

. . . .

. . . .

. . . .

. . . .

. . . .

. . . .

. . . .

. . . .

THE LAST STAND

One day I went to the house of Shemaiah son of Delaiah, the son of Mehetabel, who was shut in at his home. He said, "Let us meet in the house of God, inside the temple, and let us close the temple doors, because men are coming to kill you—by night they are coming to kill you." But I said, "Should a man like me run away? Or should someone like me go into the temple to save his life? I will not go!" I realized that God had not sent him, but that he had prophesied against me because Tobiah and Sanballat had hired him. He had been hired to intimidate me so that I would commit a sin by doing this, and then they would give me a bad name to discredit me. Remember Tobiah and Sanballat, my God, because of what they have done; remember also the prophet Noadiah and how she and the rest of the prophets have been trying to intimidate me.

-Nehemiah 6:10-14

A man Nehemiah respected advised him to take refuge in the temple because Nehemiah's life was in danger. Nehemiah was crucial to the ongoing work, and any harm to him would seriously hamper the work of rebuilding the wall. At first blush, it seemed like a wise thing to do. The president of a country is normally protected at all costs. We even have a story in the Bible about David who became tired and was almost killed in battle. His men prevented him from going to any other battles after that "so that the lamp of Israel will not be extinguished" (2 Samuel 21:17). It should not have been wrong if he protected himself.

A closer examination would yield different conclusions. There had been multiple threats to the people as they built. The Israelites were all carrying weapons and being vigilant to watch for the enemy. Nehemiah found it difficult to justify why he should stay in the safety of the temple while the people faced the threat of death daily. Hiding in the temple would mean he valued his life more than he valued theirs.

Probably more important was the place he was asked to hide. The temple was sacred, and he could not go beyond a certain point. Going into the space designated as holy and only reserved for priests would have been a sin against God. Hiding in the temple would mean he valued his life more than he valued God.

You would not expect the prophets to be on the side of their enemies. However, Nehemiah determined that Shemaiah's prophecy was not from God because it went against God's Word. Nehemiah refused to break the law even to save his life because he knew God will never lead you against His Word. Nehemiah would have lost the respect of the people he was leading and the support of the God he served because of a lack of courage.

There is a cost to following God. Sometimes it will be a matter of life and death. Most times it will be lost profits or opportunities or friends. The courage to take a stand for righteousness will preserve your integrity and give you "good" success if you hold on. Just like the Hebrew boys—Shadrach, Meshach and Abednego—who found courage, stood their ground, and refused to bow to a graven image, we must take a stand for our faith. Even though a powerful king threatened them, they chose death rather than to disobey God. Their story ended well as God chose to deliver them from the fiery furnace. It does not always end with deliverance. Sometimes a business is lost, sometimes a promotion is denied.

I must obey God even at the cost of my life. Most of us will never have to choose between our faith and death, but most of us will make choices everyday between what is sin against God and what is good. We will have a choice to be courageous rather than follow the path of least resistance. When offered a choice to run into the temple, we will say like Nehemiah did, I will not go!

"What good is it for someone to gain the whole world, yet forfeit their soul?"
 -Mark 8:36

"Shadrach, Meshach and Abednego replied to him, 'King Nebuchadnezzar, we do not need to defend ourselves before you in this matter. If we are thrown into the blazing furnace, the God we serve is able to deliver us from it, and he will deliver us from Your Majesty's hand. But even if he does not, we want you to know, Your Majesty, that we will not serve your gods or worship the image of gold you have set up.'"
 -Daniel 3:16-18

"Be strong and very courageous. Be careful to obey all the law my servant Moses gave you; do not turn from it to the right or to the left, that you may be successful wherever you go."
 -Joshua 1:7

—— Word of the Day ——
COURAGE

Mental or moral strength to venture, persevere, and withstand danger, fear, or difficulty.[28] Courage is required daily to take a stand, to make tough decisions, and to tread unproven ground. It's a huge challenge to lead other people and be responsible for their wellbeing. It's an even bigger responsibility to take the right stand when one's life is at risk. Courage is the choice to proceed in the face of opposition to fulfill the mandate given.

— What is God saying to me now? —

What choices am I avoiding because of a lack of
courage? Am I willing to pay a cost for serving God?

....
....
....
....
....
....
....
....
....
....
....
....
....
....
....
....
....
....

THE HELP OF OUR GOD

So the wall was completed on the twenty-fifth of Elul, in fifty-two days. When all our enemies heard about this, all the surrounding nations were afraid and lost their self-confidence, because they realized that this work had been done with the help of our God. Also, in those days the nobles of Judah were sending many letters to Tobiah, and replies from Tobiah kept coming to them. For many in Judah were under oath to him, since he was son-in-law to Shekaniah son of Arah, and his son Jehohanan had married the daughter of Meshullam son of Berekiah. Moreover, they kept reporting to me his good deeds and then telling him what I said. And Tobiah sent letters to intimidate me.

-Nehemiah 6:15-19

And so the wall was completed in fifty-two days! The speed at which it was completed belied the challenges Nehemiah went through as he led the people to build. Even at this time, he writes about the treachery from within that threatened the work. The nobles, the same ones he had stopped from exploiting their fellow Jews, were pledged to Tobias. While they were building, the nobles were spying and sending letters back and forth to inform Tobias of what was being done in Israel.

One wonders why these people were willing to work against their flesh and blood until Nehemiah explains they have intermarried and now had divided loyalties. Given the fact the nobles had given their daughters in marriage to Tobias and his son, there was an allegiance to them over the people of Israel. We have here a familiar tension between two valid alternatives e.g. faith and family, mercy and justice, quality and quantity.

It's not clear if the nobles were being diabolical or simply serving their selfish interests. They appeared to be trying to broker a relationship without recognizing Tobias had a different agenda. Be that as it may, the nobles did wrong in telling Tobias everything Nehemiah was saying. The nobles may have been deceived as to his true character, but Tobias's letters to intimidate Nehemiah left no doubt that Tobias was up to no good. Nehemiah now had to watch his words and actions as he dealt with the enemy within in addition to the enemy without.

During all this, the wall was still completed in fifty-two days.

Nehemiah acknowledges the help of the Lord was what enabled them to finish the work. It wasn't his skill, his political acumen, his ability to manage people, or his courage that did this. All these factors helped, but Nehemiah recognized he could not have done this by himself. The people expecting him to fail had every assurance they would stop the work. They understood the difficulty in rebuilding a wall. The city that had been defenseless for over fifty years was suddenly protected in less than two months. How does this make sense?

The Israelites spent a good portion of the time keeping watch for their enemies. They had to sift through burned stones to find materials to build the wall. All they had going for them was people willing to build and the recognition the "gracious hand of God" was on them. The help of the Lord did not take away the danger, the huge pile of rubble, the fatigue, or the ridicule.

I would go so far as to say the opposition they faced was what drove the speed at which the wall was completed. While all that was going on, the help of God gave strength to build so that everyone could see what happens when God's hand is on a people. Nehemiah did the improbable because he realized the help of the Lord will help you achieve great things!

"Now to him who is able to do immeasurably more than all we ask or imagine, according to his power that is at work within us."
 -Ephesians 3:20

"Uzziah provided the entire army with shields, spears, helmets, coats of mail, bows, and sling stones. And he built structures on the walls of Jerusalem, designed by experts to protect those who shot arrows and hurled large stones from the towers and the corners of the wall. His fame spread far and wide, for the LORD gave him marvelous help, and he became very powerful."
 -2 Chronicles 26:14-15 NLT

"With your help I can advance against a troop; with my God I can scale a wall."
 -2 Samuel 22:30

──Word of the Day──
DISTINCTION

Excellence that sets someone or something apart from others.[29] Distinction is what sets one apart from other people. It's the edge, the competitive advantage over others that separates one from the crowd. The help of God is what distinguishes us from those who do not have God.

— What is God saying to me now? —

Where do I currently need to ask for the help of God?

....

....

....

....

....

....

....

....

....

....

....

....

....

....

....

....

....

....

TIP OF THE ICEBERG

"Remember me for this, my God, and do not blot out what I have so faithfully done for the house of my God and its services."
Nehemiah 13:14

"Then I commanded the Levites to purify themselves and go and guard the gates in order to keep the Sabbath day holy. Remember me for this also, my God, and show mercy to me according to your great love."
Nehemiah 13:22

"I also made provision for contributions of wood at designated times, and for the firstfruits. Remember me with favor, my God."
Nehemiah 13:31

Nehemiah had a vision to rebuild Jerusalem. He finished the wall in fifty-two days but continued as governor for twelve years. I do not think Nehemiah could have imagined his new career while he was serving wine to the king. He only knew after the wall went up that the task of rebuilding Jerusalem went beyond the walls and gates. The wall was a very small part of all that God had in store for him, but it got him to Jerusalem.

Sometimes God reveals bigger things to us as we do the little He has already shown us. Like Abraham's servant said, *"I, being in the way, the LORD led me" (Genesis 24:27 KJV)*. The cupbearer was always a governor, but he did not know it.

The disgrace and trouble in Jerusalem was not completely resolved just because they now had a secure city. The nobles had conspired with the enemy. The temple and prophets' integrity had been compromised. Jerusalem was headed down the same path that had led to its destruction in the same place. Rebuilding was more than a physical structure, it had to do with turning the hearts of the people back to God.

Nehemiah went on to put in structure and appoint leaders through Jerusalem. He carried out a census and directed the rebuilding of houses in the city. He worked with Ezra to teach the people the law and reinstated the long-abandoned festivals. The people repented of sin and made a public vow to serve the Lord. He corrected injustice and ruled the city with integrity. The temple was cleansed, Levites were appointed, and the storehouse was full again. Nehemiah achieved all this and more because he dared to believe a cupbearer could make a difference in rebuilding the wall in Jerusalem.

Even after this great feat and all that Nehemiah did for the city, one thing stood out from Nehemiah's account of what he accomplished in the city. He wanted to be remembered most for his work in the house of God. Beyond building the wall, he wanted God to remember he had cleaned out the temple and made the Sabbath holy. Nehemiah understood that only what you do for Christ will last. Just like David was remembered as a man after God's heart, Moses as the meekest man on earth, and John as the disciple Jesus loved, Nehemiah wanted to be remembered as the man who reinstated worship in Jerusalem.

Nehemiah showed us that when God puts a burden on our hearts, it's a sign we have what it takes to make a difference. Start doing what God showed you and He will show you more. Remember that who you are now is preparing you for what you will become. So the next time your heart is broken by something, go seek God's face and know His heart's desire. Be bold and do what God has called you to do. Step out in faith and watch God do the impossible through you!

"So we make it our goal to please him, whether we are at home in the body or away from it. For we must all appear before the judgment

seat of Christ, so that each of us may receive what is due us for the things done while in the body, whether good or bad."
 -2 Corinthians 5:9-10

"Do not store up for yourselves treasures on earth, where moths and vermin destroy, and where thieves break in and steal. But store up for yourselves treasures in heaven, where moths and vermin do not destroy, and where thieves do not break in and steal. For where your treasure is, there your heart will be also."
 -Matthew 6:19-21

"A good name is more desirable than great riches; to be esteemed is better than silver or gold."
 -Proverbs 22:1

—— **Word of the Day** ——

LEGACY

Something handed over from an ancestor or predecessor or from the past.[30] My legacy is the list of things attributed to me. It is what future generations will say I accomplished. I intend to live a legacy of faith so that when all is said and done about all that I may have been graced to do, the piece that remains in people's consciousness is I served God with every part of my life!

— **What is God saying to me now?** —

What do you want others to remember you for?

. . . .
. . . .
. . . .
. . . .
. . . .
. . . .
. . . .
. . . .
. . . .
. . . .
. . . .
. . . .
. . . .
. . . .
. . . .
. . . .
. . . .
. . . .
. . . .
. . . .

CONCLUSION

And so we come to the end of this study of Nehemiah as it pertains to building the wall. Thank you for coming on this journey with me. I have personally learned a lot about studying God's Word and listening to what He is saying to me at every time. I am amazed at how the Scriptures jump out to me and how I see this with fresh eyes.

As I studied, there were good days and bad days. There were times when I forced myself to maintain the discipline of writing even when it did not seem like I was getting any revelation from God. Some other days, I would be writing as fast as I could to capture what God was pouring in my spirit. I write this to encourage you to study God's Word in the good days and the bad.

Like Nehemiah, I felt the nudge to share, and I have prayerfully written this study and now release it to the world. This study is the culmination of multiple books I have read on Nehemiah and Ezra over the past few years. Nothing I have studied has been wasted, but I have drawn out of the wells of knowledge built over the years.

I pray it has been a blessing to you. I encourage you to come back multiple times to read the nuggets you have captured under the notes. Prayerfully ask God to show you what He wants you to do. There is no downside to obeying God. He will lead, He will help, and He will uphold. Go where God says go. Do what God says do. Build a wall! Save a city! Do the impossible!

God bless you!

NOTES

. . . .
. . . .
. . . .
. . . .
. . . .
. . . .
. . . .
. . . .
. . . .
. . . .
. . . .
. . . .
. . . .
. . . .
. . . .
. . . .
. . . .
. . . .
. . . .
. . . .
. . . .
. . . .
. . . .

END NOTES

[1]"Identity." Cambridge English Dictionary.
https://dictionary.cambridge.org/dictionary/english/identity.
Accessed May 21, 2020.

[2]"Opportunity." Merriam-Webster.
https://www.merriam-webster.com/dictionary/opportunity.
Accessed May 22, 2020.

[3]"Passion." Merriam-Webster.
https://www.merriam-webster.com/dictionary/passion.
Accessed May 22, 2020.

[4]"Covenant." Holman Bible Dictionary.
https://www.studylight.org/dictionaries/hbd/c/covenant.html?hil
ite=covenant.
Accessed May 21, 2020.

[5]"Vision." Holman Bible Dictionary.

https://www.studylight.org/dictionaries/hbd/v/vision.html?hilite =vision.
Accessed May 21, 2020.

[6]"Grace." Baker's Evangelical Dictionary of Biblical Theology. Bible Study Tools.
https://www.biblestudytools.com/dictionaries /bakers-evangelical-dictionary/grace.html.
Accessed May 22, 2020.
[7]"Chesed." "Definition of God's Grace." All About...
https://www.allaboutgod.com/definition-of-gods-grace-faq.htm.
Accessed May 21, 2020.

[8]Ibid.

[9]Bill Mugavin. "4 Leadership Tips to Inspire a Shared Vision." Flash Point Leadership. March 8, 2018.
https://www.flashpointleadership.com/blog/leadership-tips-inspire-a-shared-vision.

[10]"Priorities." Collins English Dictionary.
https://www.collinsdictionary.com/dictionary/english/priorities.
Accessed May 21, 2020.

[11]https://www.ancient.eu/amorite/

[12]"Unity." King James Bible Dictionary.
http://www.kingjamesbibledictionary.com/Dictionary/unity.
Accessed May 21, 2020.

[13]"Inclusion." Cambridge English Dictionary.
https://dictionary.cambridge.org/dictionary/english/inclusion.
Accessed May 21, 2020.

[14]"Zeal."
https://www.studylight.org/dictionaries/kjd/z/zeal.html. Accessed
May 21, 2020.

[15]"Attitude." Bible Gateway Encyclopedia.
https://www.biblegateway.com/resources/encyclopedia-of-the-
bible/Attitude.
Accessed May

[16] "Organization." English Oxford Living Dictionaries.
https://www.lexico.com/en/definition/organization.
Accessed May 21, 2020.

[17] "Affirmation." Your Dictionary.
https://www.yourdictionary.com/affirmation.
Accessed May 21, 2020.

[18]"Resilience." Merriam-Webster Dictionary.
https://www.merriam-webster.com/dictionary/resilience.
Accessed May 21, 2020.

[19]"Strategy." English Oxford Living Dictionaries.
https://www.lexico.com/en/definition/strategy/
Accessed May 27, 2020.

[20] "Transparency." Wikipedia.
https://en.m.wikipedia.org/wiki/Transparency_(behavior)
Accessed May 21, 2020.

[21] "Compassion." Merriam-Webster.
https://www.merriam-webster.com/dictionary/compassion.
Accessed May 21, 2020.

[22]"H3372 – yare' – Strong's Hebrew Lexicon (NIV)." Blue Letter
Bible.
https://www.blueletterbible.org//lang/lexicon/lexicon.cfm?Stron
gs=H3372&t=NIV
Accessed 22 May, 2020.

[23] "H3374 – yir'ah – Strong's Hebrew Lexicon (NIV)." Blue Letter
Bible.

https://www.blueletterbible.org//lang/lexicon/lexicon.cfm?Stron
gs=H3374&t=NIV
Accessed 22 May, 2020.

[24] "G5401 - phobos – Strong's Greek Lexicon (NIV)." Blue Letter
Bible.
https://www.blueletterbible.org//lang/lexicon/lexicon.cfm?Stron
gs=G5401&t=NIV
Accessed 22 May, 2020.
[25] "Integrity." English Oxford Living Dictionaries.
https://www.lexico.com/en/definition/integrity. Accessed May 21,
2020.

[26] "Sacrifice." English Oxford Living Dictionaries.
https://www.lexico.com/en/definition/sacrifice.
Accessed May 21, 2020.

[27] "Focus." English Oxford Living Dictionaries.
https://www.lexico.com/en/definition/focus.
Accessed May 21, 2020.

[28] "Courage." Merriam-Webster.
https://www.merriamwebster.com/dictionary/courage.
Accessed May 22, 2020.

[29] "Distinction." English Oxford Living Dictionaries. https://www.lexico.com/en/definition/distinction. Accessed May 21, 2020.

[30] "Legacy." The Free Dictionary. https://www.thefreedictionary.com/legacy. Accessed May 21,

MEET ROTIMI IYUN

Rotimi Iyun came to faith at the tender age of nine. She holds a doctorate in theology and is a certified John Maxwell Speaker and Coach. Her writings have been featured in various magazines. She is the author of Wait Is not a Four-letter Word—a book written to encourage single women to reach for God's best. She is a speaker at women's conferences and recently released a worship album called "God my God."

Rotimi will often be found with her nose in a book (actually her Kindle), running through an airport to catch a flight or singing on the worship team in her church. She currently lives in the United States where she works as a management consultant with a leading consulting firm. You can reach Rotimi at the following social media handles

Email: timi@rotimiiyun.com
Facebook: Rotimi Iyun, Author| Instagram: Rotimiiyun | Twitter: Rotimiiyun
Website: www.rotimiiyun.com

Made in the USA
Monee, IL
06 April 2022